Urban Environmental Landscape

Edited by Dieter Grau

Publishing

Published in Australia in 2015 by
The Images Publishing Group Pty Ltd
ABN 89 059 734 431
6 Bastow Place, Mulgrave, Victoria 3170, Australia
Tel: +61 3 9561 5544 Fax: +61 3 9561 4860
books@imagespublishing.com
www.imagespublishing.com

Copyright © The Images Publishing Group Pty Ltd 2015
The Images Publishing Group Reference Number: 1186

All rights reserved. Apart from any fair dealing for the purposes of private study, research, criticism or review as permitted under the Copyright Act, no part of this publication may be reproduced, stored in a retrieval system or transmitted in any form by any means, electronic, mechanical, photocopying, recording or otherwise, without the written permission of the publisher.

National Library of Australia Cataloguing-in-Publication entry

Title:	Urban Environmental Landscape / Dieter Grau (ed.).
ISBN:	9781864706307 (hardback)
Subjects:	Landscape architecture.
	Urban landscape architecture.
	Landscape design.
	City planning.
	Architecture—Environmental aspects.

Dewey Number: 712

Coordinated and edited by Images Publishing, Shanghai office.

Printed by Toppan Leefung Printing (Shenzhen) Co. Ltd

IMAGES has included on its website a page for special notices in relation to this and our other publications. Please visit www.imagespublishing.com.

Every effort has been made to trace the original source of copyright material contained in this book. The publishers would be pleased to hear from copyright holders to rectify any errors or omissions.

The information and illustrations in this publication have been prepared and supplied by the contributor/s. While all reasonable efforts have been made to ensure accuracy, the publishers do not, under any circumstances, accept responsibility for errors, omissions and representations, express or implied.

Content

3	**Content**
6	**Preface**

Chapter 1 Public Park Design

8	1. Types of Urban Public Parks
	1.1 Special Parks
	1.2 Joint Use Parks
	1.3 Maintenance Assessment District (MAD) Parks
	1.4 Open Space Parks
8	2. Park Design Standards
9	2.1 Site Planning
	2.2 Grading and Drainage
10	2.3 Paving, Walkways, and Mow Curbs
11	2.4 Trails
	2.5 Fencing and Walls
12	2.6 Parking Areas
	2.7 Trash Enclosures
	2.8 Site Furniture
13	2.9 Signs
14	2.10 Prefabricated Picnic Shelters
	2.11 Irrigation
15	2.12 Planting
16	2.13 Synthetic Turf
18	Grand Park
30	"Paseo de la Mujer" Memorial Park
36	An Esplanade Leading to the Sea
42	Beiqijia Technology Business District
54	Footscray Park Memorial Garden
60	Fortress Ehrenbreitstein, Coblenz, Germany
66	Sishane Park
74	Ulus Savoy Housing
80	Zelaieta Park
90	Sarona Urban Park

Chapter 2 Public Plaza Design

96	1. Design Principles of Public Plaza Design
	1.1 History, Tradition, and Character
	1.2 Activity and Sociability
	1.3 Comfort and Appearance
97	2. Public Plaza Design Standards
	2.1 Dimensions
	2.2 Configuration
	2.3 Locational Restrictions
	2.4 Restrictions on Orientation
	2.5 Visibility
98	2.6 Minor Portions
	2.7 Regulations for Through Block Public Plazas
	2.8 Sidewalk Frontages
	2.9 Elevation
99	2.10 Steps
	2.11 Circulation Paths
	2.12 Permitted Obstructions
100	3. Public Plaza Design Elements
	3.1 Seating
101	3.2 Planting and Trees
102	3.3 Lighting and Electrical Power
	3.4 Litter Receptacles
	3.5 Bicycle Parking
103	3.6 Public Space Signage
	3.7 Additional Amenities
104	Dandenong Civic Centre
114	Reconstruction of the Square in Frýdlant
118	Hoekenrode Square
124	Leyteire Courtyard
130	Mechelen Centrumimpuls
138	Place d'Austerlitz in Strasbourg
144	Golden Gate Bridge 75th Anniversary Plaza Considerations

Chapter 3 Waterfront Public Open Space Design

150	1. Basic Principles and Functions for Waterfront Design
	1.1 Create a Waterfront for All
	1.2 Put the Shoreline and Innovative, Sustainable Design at the Forefront
150	2. Design Requirements for Waterfront Public Access Areas
	2.1 General Provisions Applying to Waterfront Public Access Areas
151	2.2 Design Requirements for Shore Public Walkways and Supplemental Public Access Areas
153	2.3 Design Requirements for Public Access on Piers and Floating Structures
	2.4 Public Access Design Reference Standards
158	Mulini Beach
170	Aalborg Waterfront – Linking Port & City
184	Anglet South Coastline
192	Harbour Bath and Blue Base
202	Lands End Lookout Visitors Center
206	Clock Tower beach

Chapter 4 Urban Street Design

218	1. Basic Principles of Urban Street Design
	1.1 Design Streets for Multiple People
	1.2 Great Streets Are Great for Business
	1.3 Design for Efficiency, Safety and Convenience
	1.4 Streets Can Be Changed
218	2. Basic Elements of Urban Street Design
	2.1 Lane
219	2.2 Sidewalks
220	2.3 Transit Streets
221	2.4 Stormwater Management
222	3. Urban Street Design Guide
	3.1 Intersections
223	3.2 Intersection Design Elements
226	IBK
232	Pasing Centre
238	Parc Hydro-Quebec
244	Noosa Junction Station

252	**Index**

Preface

Dieter Grau
Partner of Atelier Dreiseitl
Landscape Architect

As economic growth in Asian cities has drawn residents from the countryside into major cities, creating an accelerated wave of urbanization, by 2050, it is estimated that two-thirds of all the people in the developing world will live in cities. While there are many benefits to living in cities, cities are increasingly crowded and noisy, make people believe that they are living in reinforced concrete. In the fast-paced modern life, people are suffering unprecedented pressure both physically and psychologically. As a subject of integrating psychology, ergonomics, architectonics, and aesthetics, landscape design has become an important platform for people to sense, experience, and interact with the external world.

High quality landscape design means to creating beautiful and comfortable living space while maximize its functional satisfaction by diverse user groups. We think that public spaces should offer multiple options for use instead of the rigid programming for certain use, evoking movement beyond their physical borders. Landscape design plays a unique and important role in environmental planning and public visual interaction. It can build a distinguishable image or local characteristics as the landmark for a certain place, promote the value of commercial development projects, combine human beings and the environment together, as well as arousing people's mutual feeling for art and nature.

Cities are made up of numerous elements, including walkable streets, the vibrant waterfront landscape, public parks for residents to relax and the urban square to make people engage in activities outdoor. In terms of urban environmental landscape design, all the public open spaces, such as parks, river corridors, plazas, or other urban spaces, they have to fulfill more and more essential functions for providing lively experience for people. This could be offered in multifunctional places where citizens express themselves in various ways and perform different activities. Individualization of society is increasing and therefore spaces in cities have to be multicultural and multifunctional. Besides, landscape design has to adapt to climate change and being involved in framework of blue-green infrastructure with resilient design in City district scale. Successful urban landscape design works not only meet the various needs of popular activities outdoors, but also can be used as a communication link between humans and nature. To make people get close to nature and feel the breath of nature through public green areas.

Developing livable ecological solutions with respect to cultural and social fabric of the city is a key driver for our thinking. More and more people to aspire to the combination of nature and humanity, advocating the harmony of man and nature. Landscape designers around the world began to link their mission with the earth's ecological system. Landscape designers have certainly changed the traditional role putting the topic of interdisciplinary working style for smart urban inventions in big and small scale high on the agenda. Coping with engineers driven infrastructure and contributing in the planning process with sufficient input will be crucial to integrate soft factors into hard infrastructure of new and old cities. The core field to create beautiful, atmospheric, people-friendly urban environments will still be the key to raise people's excitement for city spaces with the goal to foster social stability in our extreme-dense and fast growing cities.

The book Urban Environmental Landscape is composed of four significant constituent parts of the urban public space – parks, squares, waterfront space, and urban streets. It includes 27 high quality urban landscape design cases from all over the world. All of the excellent projects are carefully designed to cater different clients' demands. It is a book contain many wonderful photos, site plans, or other design drawings, as well as the authoritative design standards for reference. Clock Tower Beach, Dandenong Civic Centre, Sarona Urban Park, Grand Park and Mulini Beach are all perfect projects to make people feel the unique charm of the urban landscape. For professional designers or design teams, this book definitely has a high value for reference. Designers can learn not only the newest and best design cases from this book, but also professional design design standards and trends. All of these can promote designers' abilities in their future career. It is my honor to be involved in the editing work of this book and to guide readers to appreciate the essence of urban environmental landscape design. And we hope to turn our cities into a more beautiful and livable space by logical, feasible, artistic, and innovative design.

Chapter 1 Public Park Design

Parks, recreation areas, and other open spaces enhance the quality of life for residents, workers, and visitors. Parks provide community and environmental benefits, and can also add economic value to surrounding properties. Some of the most prestigious neighborhoods in the world are located near highly renowned parks.

Along with the streetscape, parks provide locations where the public interacts and socializes. As such, it is important that high-quality parks are provided in the appropriate size, location, and type to address the needs of the community.

1. Types of Urban Public Parks

1.1 Special Parks

Special Parks are smaller than community or neighborhood parks (two acres or smaller) and contain passive recreation activities. These parks are sometimes called 'Pocket Parks', Renaissance Parks or 'Mini-Parks', and are often built by a Developer as a condition of a Land Development Permit and then turned over to the City to maintain. Walkways, trails, benches, shade structures, and small play areas are typical amenities of these parks.

1.2 Joint Use Parks

Joint use parks are found adjacent to a population-based park and a school, or may be found adjacent to a school only. The costs of land, development, and maintenance are shared equally by the City and the school district. Joint use parks are designed and constructed to the standards of the Consultant's Guide when the City will be responsible for long-term maintenance. A Joint Use Agreement between the City and the school district will be processed by the City.

1.3 Maintenance Assessment District (MAD) Parks

Maintenance Assessment District (MAD) parks are special parks that are maintained through an assessment of nearby property owners that is levied annually. Maintenance assessment districts maintain a variety of landscaping features, including certain parks and streetscapes. In cases where a maintenance assessment district maintains a park, typically the additional park is above the city's standard identified in the General Plan. Most maintenance assessment districts also maintain streetscapes, which typically include enhanced improvements along a public right of way, including street trees, greenbelt landscaping, center median landscaping, planted slopes, decorative benches and trash receptacles, decorative paving, enhanced street lighting, and trails that are typically adjacent to public rights-of-way.

1.4 Open Space Parks

Open space parks are land which is owned by the city consisting of canyons, mesas, and other natural landforms. Open space parks are intended to preserve and protect native plants and animals while providing public access and enjoyment by the use of hiking, biking, and equestrian trails. Open space parks generally have minimal development and are intended to remain in their natural state.

2. Park Design Standards

The following design standards address functional and aesthetic issues for park and open space design, and are to be referenced and utilized during the formulation of General Development Plans and final Construction Plans. All parks and open space shall meet the following guidelines and regulations.

2.1 Site Planning

Park design and site planning shall include analysis and integration of on-site and off-site features such as bicycle and pedestrian trails, open space areas, topography, views, existing vegetation and joint-use needs of adjacent schools. Community Plans, Master or Precise Plans, General Development Plans, and other City planning documents shall be referenced when analyzing and evaluating the project during site planning. (Refer to table 1.1)

2.2 Grading and Drainage

(1) Grade

All park projects shall have positive drainage and provide the necessary components for drainage. Drainage is to be directed away from buildings, electrical enclosures, backstops, and irrigation controllers. The following gradients shall be used in preparing grading and drainage plans.

(2) Drainage Systems

Drainage systems shall be designed and sized per flow requirements and engineered accordingly. Drainage systems shall conform to the City's Grading Development Regulations and Drainage Regulations.

(3) Storm Water Run-off and Best Management Practices

All park projects shall be designed to meet requirements of the City's Municipal Code and the Storm Water Standards Section of the Land Development Manual. Bio-swales, permeable paving, and other natural means of filtration of storm water run-off are preferred to mechanical means; the use of storm ceptors and similar technologies is discouraged.

Table 1.1 Gradients Used in Preparing Grading and Drainage Plans

Use	Grade
Walkways and Pedestrian Paving: Pedestrian walkways and monolithic surfaces of concrete, asphalt or unit pavers	1.5% minimum, 4.5% maximum. 1.5% maximum cross slope, no exceptions. Paving outside of street rights-of-way shall meet current Title 24 and ADA accessibility guidelines.
Basketball and Volleyball Courts: Multi-purpose paved courts	Drain end-to-end at 1%.
Tennis Courts	Drain side-to-side or end-to-end at 1%. Never allow high point at net.
Multi-purpose Fields	1.5% minimum, 2% maximum.
Softball and Baseball Fields	1.5% for skinned and turf infields. 1.5% for turf outfields. Provide positive drainage away from home plate in all cases.
Parking Areas: Asphalt	1% minimum, 4% maximum with a 4.5% maximum cross slope. 1.5% maximum slope in any direction where accessible parking is required, no exceptions.
Turf Areas: Passive recreation	2% minimum, 20% (5:1) maximum.
Shrub and Groundcover Areas	2% minimum, 50% (2:1) maximum.
Mulch Areas	2% minimum, 20% (5:1) maximum.
Unpaved Trails	Developed parks: 1.5% minimum, 4.5% maximum. 1.5% maximum cross slope, no exceptions.

2.3 Paving, Walkways, and Mow Curbs

(1) Paving and Walkway Designs

Walkways are provided in all parks for functional and aesthetic purposes. Functionally, walkways should provide connections to different parts of the park and lead to special landmarks. Walkways that provide a loop system are preferred. Primary walkways in the park shall be concrete paving without color. At park perimeter(s) and parking lots, walkways should be located to provide a logical, convenient, and aesthetic means of accessing the park. Walkways shall be accessible to all users. Aesthetically, walkways should be designed to allow the user to enjoy on and off-site views, and the different amenities of the park.

(2) Walkway Locations

Where possible provide walkways to separate turf areas from shrub and groundcover areas to reduce edging costs.

(3) Walkway Widths

Primary pedestrian / maintenance access walkways and security lighting: nine feet wide minimum.

Walkways adjacent to ball field lights: 12 feet wide minimum.

Walkways adjacent to parking stalls without wheel stops: nine feet wide minimum.

Secondary pedestrian walkways without maintenance access or security lighting: six feet wide minimum.

(4) Walkway Construction

Walkway construction and reinforcement shall be based on the geotechnical report prepared specifically for the project. Geotechnical testing shall be provided during the design phase and shall be included in the bid documents. When no geotechnical report is available, walkways shall be constructed in accordance with the San Diego Standard Drawings and Greenbook specifications.

Walkways that are required to support maintenance vehicles shall be clearly identified on the plans and designed to support maintenance vehicles. The minimum thickness shall be six inches for these walkways. Walkways adjacent to ball field lights and site security lights shall be designed to meet this criterion.

(5) Unpaved Walkways

Unpaved walkways may be proposed as a secondary component of a park's circulation system. These walkways shall be stabilized decomposed granite, pre-mixed by the plant at the rate recommended by the manufacturer, prior to delivery. A weed barrier is recommended below all decomposed granite paving. The preferred walkway edging is concrete, non-corrosive metal or recycled plastic lumber (Trex or equal). Edging adjacent to turf areas shall be concrete.

(6) Mow Curbs

Concrete mow curbs shall be provided to separate all turf areas from shrub, groundcover or mulch areas, to contain decomposed granite paving, under fencing adjacent to turf or groundcover that requires edging or mowing, and as an integral component of any wall (both at the top and bottom) where turf is proposed or exists. Mow curb width shall be eight inches minimum, 16 inches minimum beneath fences.

2.4 Trails

Trails provide for the use of alternative modes of transportation, as well as recreational activities. The various trail components include pedestrian, bicycling, and equestrian trails. Trails shall be designed in compliance with the Park and Recreation Department's Trail Policies and Standards.

2.5 Fencing and Walls

Parks shall be designed functionally and visually as open as possible with as little fencing as possible. Fencing shall only be provided for multipurpose fields, joint use areas or where there is a safety issue that cannot be reasonably addressed by some other means. Fencing may be used where a lot is in close proximity to streets, parking lots, or other high volume vehicular use areas that pose a safety concern. For security reasons, solid fencing shall not be used.

(1) Ornamental Fencing

Ornamental fencing shall be used to maintain views or to be consistent with a project's design theme. All components shall be tubular steel or heavy duty aluminum. Tubular steel components shall be hot dip galvanized after fabrication (free of burrs and sharp edges). Steel posts and rails shall be minimum 14-gauge, and steel pickets shall be minimum 16-gauge. Fence color shall be a powder coated paint applied electrostatically.

(2) Chain-Link Fencing

Chain link fencing may vary in height and detailing as per the specific site use(s) and requirements. If a fence exceeds eight feet in height a mid-rail will be required. Chain link fabric shall be located on the side adjacent to play or use areas.

(3) Gates

Pedestrian gates shall be a minimum of four feet wide. Gates for maintenance vehicles shall be a minimum of 12 feet wide; use double swing gates.

(4) Walls (Retaining and Free-standing)

Walls shall be designed and located to discourage skateboarding and graffiti vandalism. Walls designed to avoid the need for skate stoppers are preferred to straight walls with skate stoppers. All concrete masonry walls shall be finished with a wall cap made of precast concrete units that are sized for the block, or shall have a custom cap designed for the wall; mortar caps are not acceptable. Caps for walls less than 36 inches in height and adjacent to walkways or turf areas shall have radiused or chamfered edges for safety.

Retaining walls shall be installed with wall drains. Guard rails or fencing shall be provided at the top of walls when walls are over

30 inches in height with turf or walkways adjacent to the top. Walls and caps shall have anti-graffiti coating applied.

2.6 Parking Areas

(1) Parking Ratio for Neighborhood Parks

Provide five parking spaces per acre of non-programmed parkland. When a neighborhood park has softball fields, provide an additional 30 parking spaces per backstop. Parking may be provided by on-site parking facilities or on adjacent streets. If parking is provided on adjacent streets, only those spaces immediately adjacent to the park may be included; parking spaces located across the street or on non-adjacent streets will not be included.

(2) Parking Ratio for Community Parks

Provide five parking spaces per acre of non-programmed parkland.

Recreation centers: One parking space per 200 square feet of building.

Swimming pool facility: One parking space per 175 square feet of pool surface area, in addition to the parking spaces required for the recreation center.

Multi-Purpose Fields: 30 parking spaces per backstop, in addition to the parking spaces required for the recreation center or swimming pool facility.

Tennis courts: 12 parking spaces per six courts, in addition to the parking spaces required for the recreation center. If less than six courts are provided, no additional parking is required.

2.7 Trash Enclosures

Trash enclosures shall be constructed with concrete masonry block. Trash enclosures shall be located within parking lot areas where feasible. Trash enclosures shall be sized to house a minimum of two dumpsters; one for trash and one for recycling. A heavy vehicle load paving section for the drive lane and the concrete apron shall be provided at the head of the enclosure. Minimum size of the concrete apron shall be sufficient to allow refuse vehicle access to the trash receptacles. Specific dimensions, location, and design shall be reviewed and approved by the Park and Recreation Department. The walls of the trash enclosure shall be treated with anti-graffiti coating inside and out. The enclosures shall have solid steel doors or chain link doors with screening slats with locking ability.

2.8 Site Furniture

All parks shall have picnic tables, benches, drinking fountains, barbecues, bicycle racks, trash receptacles, and other site furnishings as necessary. Types of site furniture selected shall be based on the type of park, design character, durability, and maintenance. Precast concrete furniture with anti-graffiti coating is preferred for durability. Site furnishings shall complement each other in color, materials, and form. Site furniture shall be permanently secured to the paving per the manufacturer's recommendations. Site furniture that bolts together is not permitted.

(1) Locations

Locate site furniture outside of turf areas whenever possible. Site furniture in turf areas shall be placed on a concrete pad with a minimum of eight inches of clearance around to accommodate mowers. Site furniture in turf areas shall be spaced a minimum of 12 feet from other site furniture, fencing, walls, lights, trees, and other vertical obstructions to accommodate City mowers. Site furniture shall be located to avoid conflicts with irrigation systems and other park improvements.

(2) Picnic Tables

Picnic tables shall be placed on concrete pads with a 1.5% maximum slope in any direction. Concrete pads shall extend four feet beyond the table / bench dimensions on all sides. The orientation of picnic tables adjacent to walkways shall be perpendicular to the path of travel to discourage skateboard activity. Picnic table configurations shall meet current accessibility standards for quantity, location, and design. One-piece tables with benches are required; deviation from this standard must be approved in writing by the Park and Recreation Department.

(3) Park Benches

Park benches shall be placed on concrete pads, and designed and located to discourage skateboard activity. When located in turf areas, the concrete pads shall provide a minimum eight inches of clearance around the perimeter to accommodate mowers. One-piece benches are required. Bench configurations shall meet current accessibility standards for quantity, location, and bench design.

(4) Drinking Fountains

Each park shall have at least one drinking fountain. Where softball backstops are included, provide one drinking fountain for each backstop or group of backstops. Where recreation centers or comfort stations are included, provide a wall-mounted drinking fountain on the exterior of the building or a pedestal style drinking fountain in the immediate vicinity. When a drinking fountain is building mounted, all plumbing shall be concealed within the walls of the building or within the plumbing chase; plumbing exposed to the public is not acceptable. All drinking fountains shall comply with current accessibility standards.

(5) Barbecues and Hot Coal Receptacles

Barbecues and hot coal receptacles shall be located outside of circulation routes. Hot coal receptacles shall be visible from the barbecue area(s). Barbecues and hot coal receptacles shall be located on a non-combustible surface such as concrete paving, stabilized decomposed granite, or turf; do not locate them, in shrub / groundcover areas or mulch areas. If located in turf areas, provide a concrete pad with a minimum of eight inches of clearance around the perimeter to accommodate mowers.

(6) Trash Receptacles

Trash receptacles shall be square and provided with a locking side opening to facilitate servicing. All trash receptacles shall have a protective 'hood' cover. Trash receptacles shall be located in paved areas or shall have their own concrete pad. Provide a minimum of eight inches of clearance around the trash receptacle when in or adjacent to turf areas to accommodate mowers.

2.9 Signs

All parks shall have at least one permanently installed park identification sign. The sign shall also be consistent with the City's corporate image policy defined in the Corporate Identity Manual. The City's seal and the Park and Recreation Department logo shall be included in the design. The sign shall harmonize with the park's theme or natural character. Signs are typically one-sided and parallel to the most prominent public street, or angled if located at the intersection of two streets. Light fixtures shall be vandal-resistant.

2.10 Prefabricated Picnic Shelters

Prefabricated picnic shelters shall be all steel construction. The finish shall be an electrostatically applied powder coat. Roofs shall be standing metal seam or similar, with no exposed screws.

2.11 Irrigation

(1) General Requirements

Irrigation system efficiency: The irrigation system for turf areas shall be designed to achieve a Distribution Uniformity (DU) of 70 percent, or 0.70. To achieve this goal, the irrigation system shall be audited by an independent Certified Landscape Irrigation Auditor, certified by the Irrigation Association. Deficiencies shall be corrected prior to the start of the Plant Establishment Period. These requirements shall be included in the construction documents.

Irrigation design: The irrigation system shall be designed utilizing water conservation standards and equipment. The irrigation design shall be based on accurate pressure information and produce an irrigation system which efficiently and uniformly applies water throughout the site. The irrigation design shall also have sufficient residual pressure and flow to accommodate site conditions, field changes, and unforeseen future demands, as well as anticipated future demands, if it is a phased project.

(2) Recycled Water

The irrigation designer shall verify the need to design the irrigation system for recycled water use with the appropriate water district. Cross connection test stations shall be a cast brass or bronze ball valve, 3/4 inch female thread, installed in a concrete valve box with a cast iron locking lid.

(3) Irrigation Controllers

Irrigation systems shall be controlled by an automatic electrical controller.

Controller locations: Controllers shall be installed at locations approved by the Park and Recreation Department. The preferred location is wall-mounted inside a Park and Recreation storage room of a comfort station, recreation center, or other permanent park building. When a comfort station, recreation center, or other park building is not present, the controller(s) shall be installed in a controller enclosure located in a shrub or mulch area; do not install irrigation controller enclosures in turf areas.

Interior mounted controllers: When located inside a Park and Recreation storage room or other acceptable space, the irrigation controller(s) shall be mounted on a pre-assembled controller and backboard assembly.

Exterior mounted controllers: When not located inside a permanent park building, irrigation controllers shall be installed in a vandal-resistant, weather-proof, stainless steel enclosure on a concrete pad.

Rain shut-off device: Provide an automatic rain shut-off device in a vandal-resistant enclosure for each controller or group of controllers. The rain shut-off device shall be located in an area subject to rainfall but out of the spray area for irrigation.

2.12 Planting (General Requirements)

Planting Design: Shall be appropriate for the site and climate conditions and shall enhance the park site and the park user's experience.

Plant Spacing and Locations: All planting shall be located to permit the proper operation of irrigation systems and the effective use of mechanized maintenance equipment. Plant locations and spacing shall permit normal plant development without undue crowding or trimming. Shrubs, groundcover, and vines shall be spaced a minimum of one-half of their mature diameter from all walkways.

Slope Revegetation: As a minimum, all existing and manufactured slopes greater than 4:1 and over five feet in vertical height shall be revegetated per the City-Wide Landscape Regulations. All other slopes shall be revegetated in accordance with park aesthetics.

Brush Management: All areas requiring brush management shall be designed per the City-Wide Landscape Regulations.

Parking Areas: All parking areas shall provide a minimum of five percent of the parking area as landscaping. Within the parking area, one 24-inch box tree shall be provided within 30 feet of each parking space. The required trees shall be located in a minimum of 40 square feet of landscape area. Parking areas adjacent to public rights-of-way shall provide a 30 inch high screen. Plants may be used to screen the parking area if the plants selected will provide a 30 inch high screen within two years. Curbs (six inch minimum height) are required to protect all landscape areas within parking areas.

Trees: Trees planted in turf areas shall be spaced to permit the most effective use of mechanized maintenance equipment and operation of the irrigation system. Trees planted in turf areas shall have a minimum of 12 horizontal feet between trees and other vertical objects. For all trees installed in turf areas, provide a 4 feet diameter mulched area around the base of the tree; there shall be no mulch on the crown of tree. Dense tree groves shall not be planted in turf areas.

Shrubs / Vines: Ornamental shrub beds in parks and around park buildings may be provided with approval from the Park and Recreation Department. Shrubs and vines adjacent to building walls shall have a mature height that preserves visual access. Provide a two inch layer of mulch in all shrub areas.

Groundcover: Shall be planted with triangular spacing at a distance that will typically ensure 100 percent coverage within one year of installation.

Turf: Turf shall be used for passive and active recreational uses. Turf areas shall be of a size and configuration to permit the most effective use of mechanized maintenance equipment and reduce edging. Small decorative turf areas are not permitted.

2.13 Synthetic Turf

(1) Application

Synthetic turf systems may be considered for use in public park facilities when intended for permitted, active sports-related recreational activities or to replace small, high use natural turf areas that are difficult to maintain as determined by the Park and Recreation Director.

(2) Installation Criteria

The synthetic turf system for athletic fields shall be a crumb rubber, crumb rubber and silica sand, synthetic or organic infill type with a subterranean drainage system sufficient to allow the playing surface to drain quickly.

The manufacturer shall have local or regional representation capable of performing repairs and providing maintenance advice in a timely manner.

Synthetic turf field intended for multi-use shall not incorporate game striping or skinned infields to allow flexibility in use. Using alternate synthetic turf colors to delineate infields, running tracks or other uses will be reviewed and approved on a case by case basis by the Park and Recreation Director. Only City-approved field marking paint or systems shall be allowed.

All components of the synthetic turf system shall meet or exceed relevant federal, state, and local health requirements. Manufacturers shall be required to fully disclose all materials used in the manufacture of the synthetic turf system and provide complete information on all potentially toxic constituents.

The project specifications for a synthetic turf system shall include provisions to secure the necessary equipment and training to properly maintain the synthetic turf system according to the manufacturer's recommendations and warrantee requirements.

A synthetic turf facility for sports-related activities shall be by permit only, unless otherwise supervised by City staff, and shall be designed to be secured when not in use.

Signs shall be posted with user health and safety guidelines at all synthetic turf fields. These signs shall include, but not be limited to, advising users how to recognize heat-related illnesses and the proper steps to take to moderate and treat such illnesses, emphasize good hygiene such as washing hands after playing and practicing, and standard first aid for skin wounds to prevent infections.

Signs shall be posted to indicate which activities are allowed and not allowed on the synthetic turf. These signs shall address, but not be limited to, items such as food, drinks, pets, and certain types of chairs, umbrellas, athletic shoes, and athletic equipment which may damage the turf and invalidate the manufacturer's warranty or shorten the product's life expectancy.

Sun shade and drinking fountains shall be provided near the synthetic turf field. Where shade and/or drinking fountains cannot be provided due to design or site constraints, efforts shall be taken to encourage users to provide acceptable portable shade systems and drinking water.

Each synthetic turf installation shall include a water system including quick coupling valves to assist in the proper maintenance of the system. Potable water shall not be used to cool the synthetic turf playing surface.

The recyclability of the synthetic turf and infill components shall be considered when selecting the synthetic turf type to ensure the materials can be recycled at the end of the useful life.

Synthetic turf fields shall not be installed in flood-prone areas due to potential damage to the turf and possible dissemination of synthetic turf materials, such as the infill material, into storm drains or natural drainage courses.

The City's Strom Water Department or Division shall review the proposed synthetic turf system during the project's design phase.

Reference:
City of San Diego, Consultant's Guide to Park Design & Development

Grand Park

Location: Bunker Hill, Downtown Los Angeles, USA
Area: 120,000m²
Completion Date: 2012
Landscape Architect: Rios Clementi Hale Studios
Photography: Tom Bonner, Jim Simmons
Client: Grand Avenue Committee; Related Companies; County of Los Angeles
Awards: Building Team Award, from The American Institute of Architects, Los Angeles Chapter, 2012
ASLA / SCC Honor Award, Design, from The American Society of Landscape Architects, Southern California Council, 2012
ASLA/SCC Merit Award, Planning and General Development, from The American Society of Landscape Architects, Southern California Council, 2010
AIA/LA NEXT LA Citation Award, from The American Institute of Architects, Los Angeles Chapter, 2010
ASLA / SCC Honor Award, Planning and Analysis, from The American Society of Landscape Architects, Southern California Council, 2007 (Grand Park Public Workshop Toolkit)

Grand Park is located on what was an underutilized urban site in downtown Los Angeles' Bunker Hill neighborhood, with 90 feet of grade change along a four-block area. Grand Avenue and The Music Center complex comprise the west border; Los Angeles City Hall and Spring Street anchor the site to the east. The site previously held the Los Angeles County Civic Center Mall a formal open space that included the Arthur J. Will Memorial Fountain, trees, and a small Starbucksas well as a surface parking lot just west of City Hall. The area, designed decades ago for ease of vehicular traffic entering a below-grade parking structure, was essentially cut off from its surroundings by vehicular ramps and large government buildings. This central site is accessible by public transit.

Different activities occur in Grand Park's four public spaces, or "blocks." In Blocks One and Two, visitors will find the Fountain Plaza with the regal, restored Arthur J. Will Memorial Fountain and interactive water features (by Fluidity Design Consultants); new buildings, which house the park office and public restrooms; Olive

Site Plan

1. Department of water and power
2. Reflecting pool
3. Access bridge
4. Ahmanson theatre
5. Mark taper forum
6. Dorothy chandler pavilion
7. Valet drop-off
8. Interactive fountain
9. Exit ramp
10. Park offices below
11. Existing crosswalk
12. ADA access
13. Location for art
14. Entrance ramp
15. Entry plaza
16. Elevator
17. Overlook plaza
18. Fountain restoration and membrane pool
19. Fountain plaza
20. ADA access
21. Stone bench
22. Starbucks building, restrooms, and support
23. Outdoor dining
24. County courts
25. Hall of administration
26. Building entry
27. Existing escalator entry
28. Olive court
29. Relocated historic benches
30. Existing escalator entry
31. Sun garden
32. Performance lawn
33. Stage
34. Promenade paving typical all blocks
35. Existing parking entrance ramp
36. Location for art
37. Existing parking exit ramp
38. Existing elevator
39. Parking structure
40. Plaza
41. Existing elevator
42. MTA portal
43. MTA plaza
44. Community terrace
45. Parking access
46. Law library
47. Hall of records
48. Loading / service
49. Bleacher seating and ADA ramp
50. Central stairs
51. Park entry
52. Relocated court of flags
53. Criminal courts building
54. New ADA parking
55. New ramp to parking
56. Dog run
57. Event lawn
58. Multi-use market place
59. Existing building foundation
60. Restroom and park support
61. City hall west steps
62. Location for art
63. City hall
64. South entry
65. South lawn

A. Hope Street
B. Grand Avenue
C. Temple Street
D. First Street
E. Broadway
F. Spring Street

In the heart of downtown Los Angeles

Court, a plaza that marks the historic alignment of Olive Street with olive trees and Mediterranean plantings, as well as historic speaker poles and benches; and the Performance Lawn with broad expanses of grass and a small stage. This shady lawn area incorporates several existing Jacaranda trees and is surrounded by various gardens containing plants from North America, Australia, and Southeast Asia.

In Blocks Three and Four, visitors will find the Community Terrace, a large central plaza surrounded by gardens from each of the world's six Floristic Kingdoms; small lawn areas for picnics and lounging; a Flag Garden; the Broadway Terraces, providing ADA access down to the street level, as well as informal stepped-seating areas; the Event Lawn, an open, flexible area for large public gatherings and marketplace; and even a dog run. Wide steps along with ADA-accessible ramps, switchback paths, and the landscape architect's reworked grades mitigate Bunker Hill's 90 feet of grade change throughout the length of the park.

Section

"Splash Pad" new interactive water feature

South Elevation

North Elevation

The restored historic Arthur J. Will Memorial Fountain

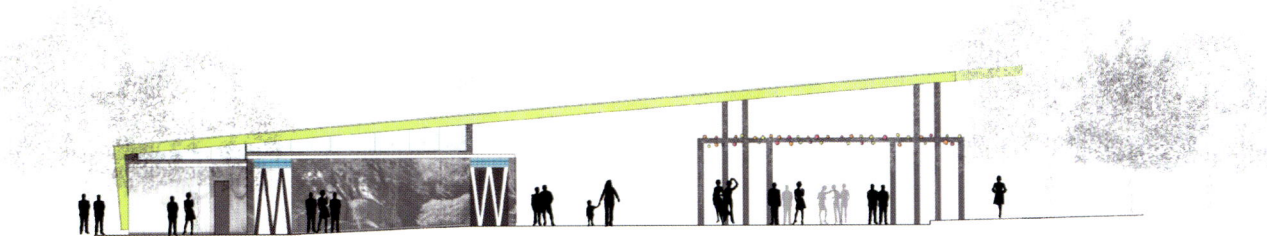

North Elevation

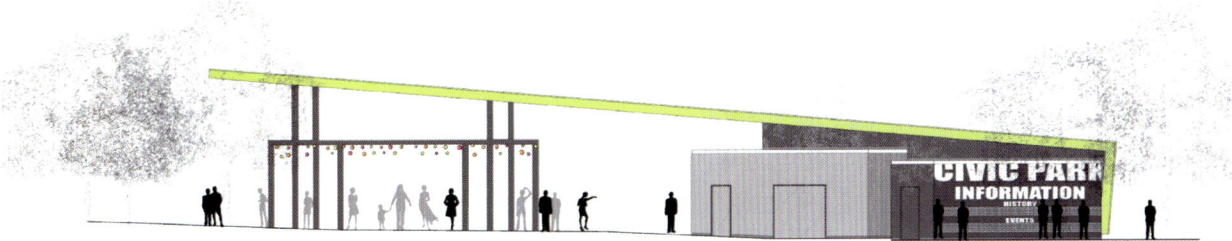

South Elevation

Top: Plant palette and garden markers indicate kingdom and region, climate, and specific characters of featured tree.
Opposite: Paths lead to the relocated court of flags.

Red Torch Ginger | Salvia | Camphor Tree | Euphorbia Characias | California Poppy | Kenya Aloe | Pink Cordyline | Red Kangaroo Paw | Swamp Banksia

Elephant Ear | King Protea | Green Aloe | Leucadendron | Chalk Dudleya | Kangaroo Paw | Heliconia | New Zealand Flax | Black Spined Agave

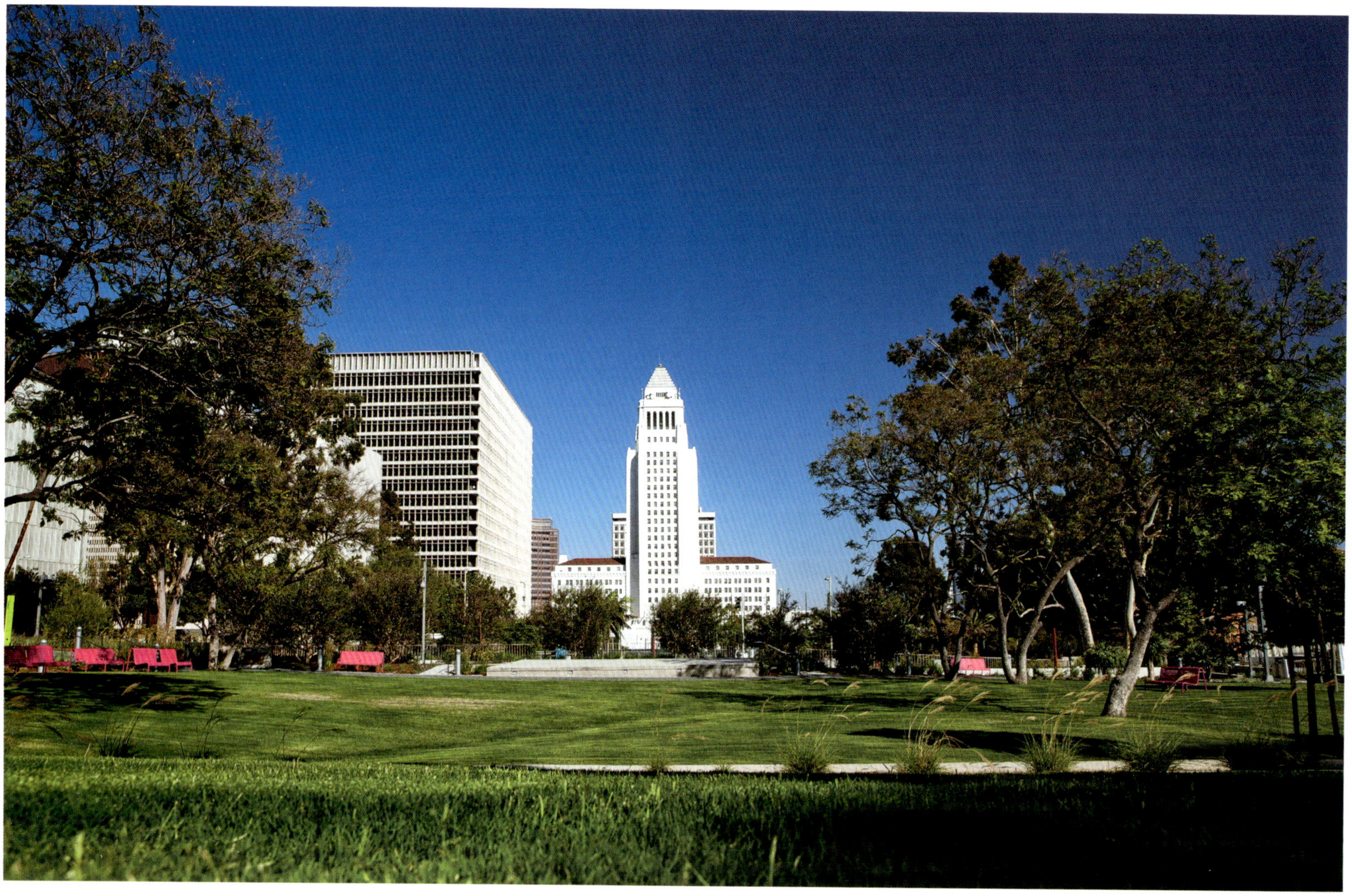

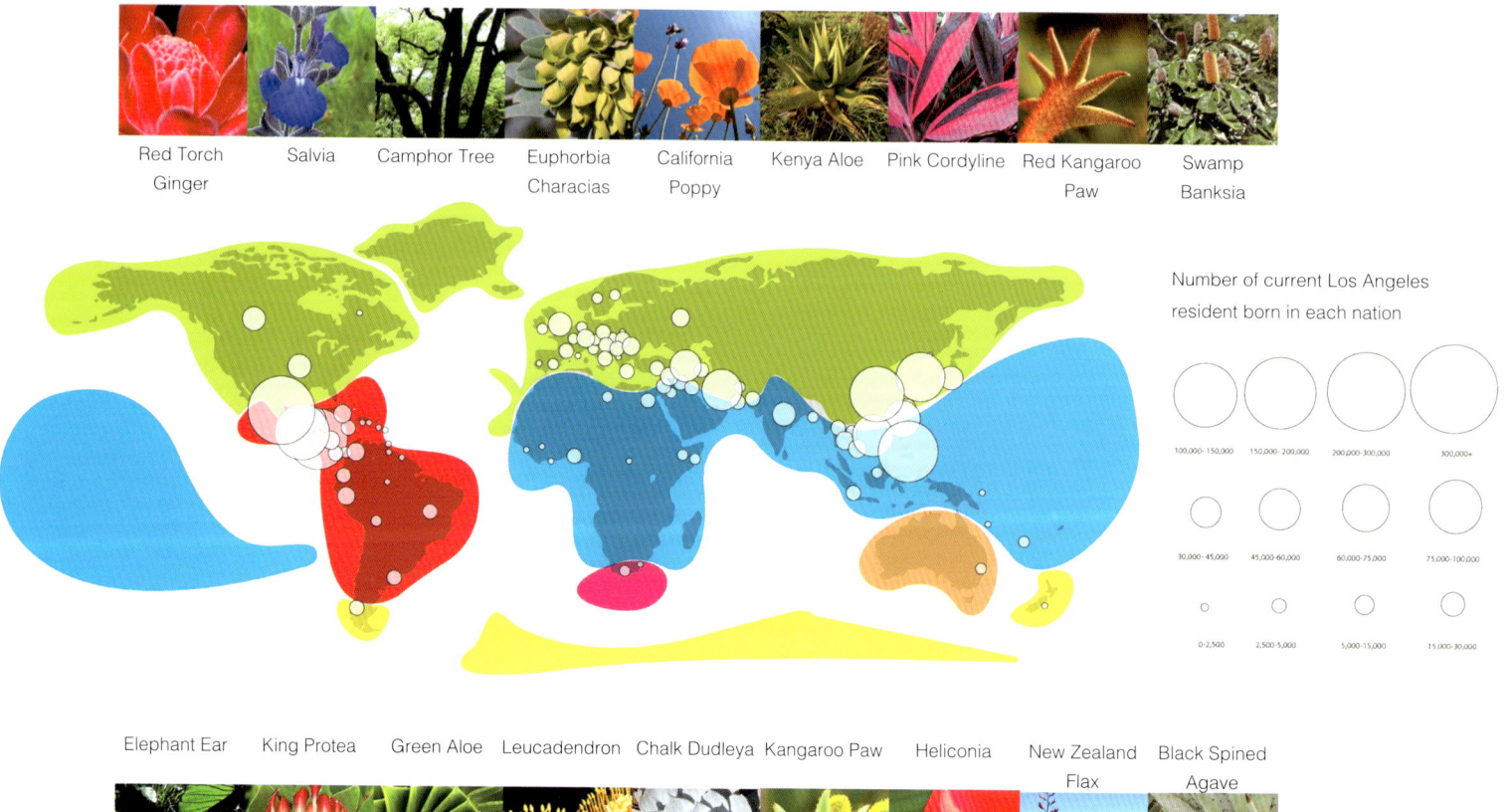

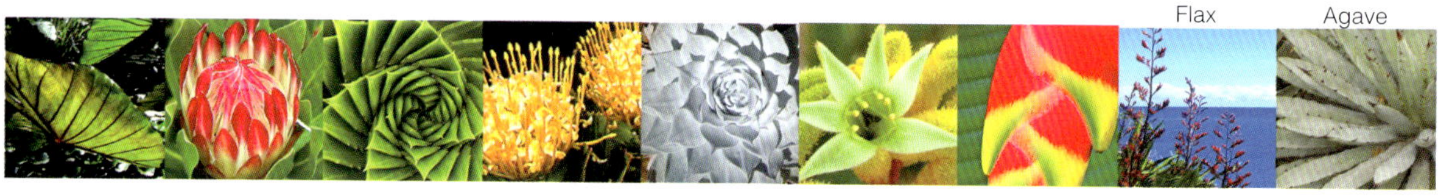

Opposite top: View of stage and City Hall from performance lawn.
Opposite bottom: Plant palette is based on floristic kingdoms.
Top: Open community spaces feature movable furniture designed for the park.
Bottom: The Olive Court features Mediterranean species.

Top: Stairs and ramps mitigate grade changes.
Opposite: A variety of pathways help all visitors navigate the park.

"Paseo de la Mujer" Memorial Park

Location: Monterrey, Mexico
Area: 17,290m²
Completion Date: 2013
Landscape Design: Susana García, DLC Architects
Photography: DLC Architects, Julio Cortéz Alvarez
Client: Vitro, "Parque Fundidora" trust, City of Monterrey N.L. México

"Paseo de la Mujer" Memorial Park was conceptualized first as an idea by the Government of Monterrey and Philanthropists, Maria Elena Melo de Sada and "El Museo del Vidrio" (The Museum of Glass), as a response to the fact that in the whole of Mexico, there was no place to remember the women who have been important in Mexico's history, from poets to rebels, from scientists to musicians.

The project is placed inside Monterrey's most important park and green area called "Parque Fundidora", close to a very important freeway and on a very steep natural slope that also served as a "natural" water drainage for the park.

The main idea was to "consolidate" the space creating a sort of "crater" to give the feeling of a more private space and a downward spiral to walk through it. The crater is "sectioned" by an axis that is formed from a "glass bridge" virtually dividing the park in two and also differentiating the types of vegetation, whereas the side of the park that is next to the freeway would be visualized more as a forest emphasizing the private quality of the park, and the other side would become a more "open" and "colored" space.

At first the "Glass Bridge" would be more of a "glass wall", which at least was the main idea. The wall would serve also as a "canvas" to project the names of the famous Mexican women and also as a more "strong" division.

The overview image

Site Plan

Section

The Park also considered a 50m tall sculpture as a destination for the "glass bridge" and also as an "urban signage" for the park.

The most important intention for the project was the ability to discover the park, having multiple options to do it, serving also as a reminder of more beautiful and complex mind every women possesses.

Another important feature that is not entirely of the landscape architecture process was that the park would be built from donations from a trust that was formed specifically for the project. External economical crises in Mexico have forced the project to be constructed very slowly.

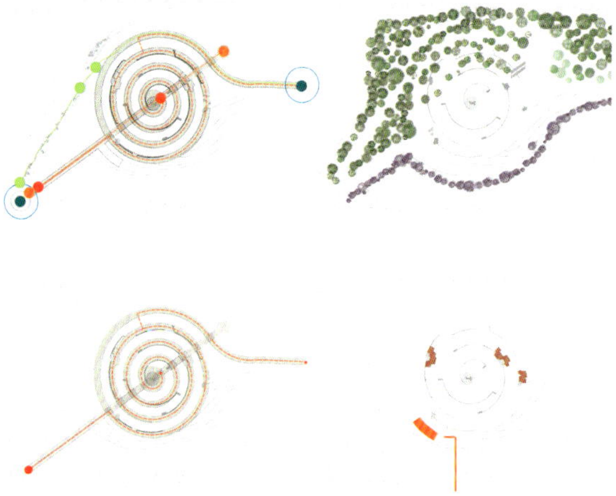

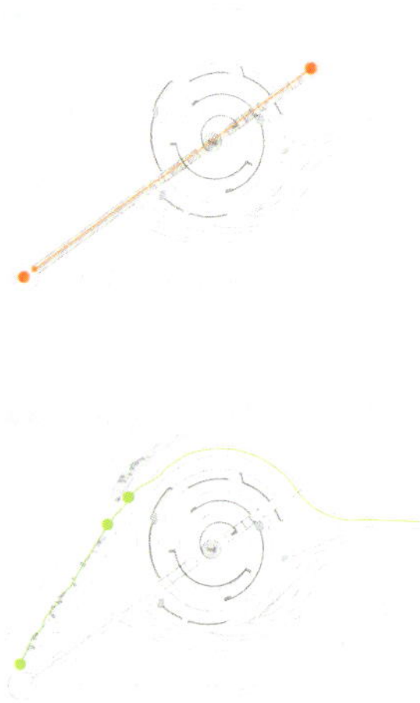

1. Cristal multimedia pavillion
2. "Crater balcony"
3. "Axis"
4. Urban sculpture
5. Cristal "Wall of Women"
6. Water=Life
7. Bigger scale vegetation on the edge of the project and lower on the crater
8. "Downnward spiral" path
9. Steep slopes
10. "Crater"

An Esplanade Leading to the Sea

Location: Quiberon, France
Area: 32,800m²
Completion Date: 2014
Landscape Design: URBICUSLtd. / Jean-Marc Gaulier
Photography: Charles Delcourt
Client: City of Quiberon

Quiberon lies on the southern point of the Brittany peninsula and tourists flock here for its beauty and nature. The ageing public spaces and heavy presence of cars didn't provide the best setting for visitors and the weekly market. Its under-promoted seaside location and three existing parks had the potential to give the city centre a new lease of life and transform it into a great setting for tourists and locals alike.

The aim of the project is to reconnect the centre and seafront by designing a large esplanade with ocean views and linking the existing parks to take walkers from the high street all the way to the beach.

The lush esplanade hosts the market and summer events in a spacious and multi-functional space. The tilework covering the ground highlights pedestrians' right of way and helps to lay out the market. The gray granite brings out the ground's design and contrasts with the region's signature yellow granite. The wooden terraces nestled in the parks dotted all over this large mineral space provide more private areas for people to take a break.

Some trees were saved to ensure plantlife remains a key feature and because part of the site is in a protected area. With the same respect for heritage, the existing stone walls have been showcased with lighting and new openings to link the different parts of the park. The existing parks were redesigned to connect the beach and town centre with three contrasting settings. The south part of the esplanade's park has plant species from the Brittany coastline's dunes to bring the beach to the town centre.

Site Plan

Section Plan of the Plant Area

Top: Overview image
Middle: Vegetation area
Opposite and bottom: The street

In the middle the plants are inspired by the Brittany moors. The plant life is more exotic in the most protected part of the park in tribute to the great voyages which Brittany's sailors went on over the centuries. This meant that several species from abroad were imported to adapt to the region's temperate climate and are the pride and joy of the Brittany parks. To raise awareness of nature conservation, there is educational signage all along the promenade.

Beiqijia Technology Business District

Location: Beijing, China
Area: 600,000m²
Completion Date: 2014
Landscape Design: Martha Schwartz Partners
Photography: Terrence Zhang
Client: Beijing Ningke Real Estate

The project is located in Changping District, Beijing, and belongs to the Beijing Technology Business District and is the first phase of the overall master plan development. The landscape site area is approximately 60,000m². The site is a mixed use development, including residential, offices, and retail.

The landscape consists of three different zones or character areas, responding to the requirements of each type of programmatic use: Commercial / Retail, Central Park, and Residential. The commercial / Retail area includes the landscapes around the Headquarters Offices, the Office Courtyard Gardens, the Qui Bei Road Promenade, and the Eco Zone Area, which is located at the very north of the site – a linear landscape with an ecological function-collecting and absorbing all the stormwater runoff from the site. This mesic habitat also provides room for seating, strolling, and one of the two the artisticgateway structures, which draw people into the green heart: the Central Park. The Central Park is an open space with the "public green" and the "sunken gardens". Here, a sunny corner garden frames the sunken lawn area with raised planters which are planted with low hedges, ornamental grasses, and perennials. Along its edges people can sit and enjoy the sun or lay down on the lounge chairs carefully positioned in the sunny spots of the gardens. The cool breeze from the central water feature would create this beach-like atmosphere in an urban setting.

Another major component of the Central Park is the central water feature, which utilizes treated rainwater to create play opportunities for the local residents and the public, as well as to separate the private residential area from the public open space.

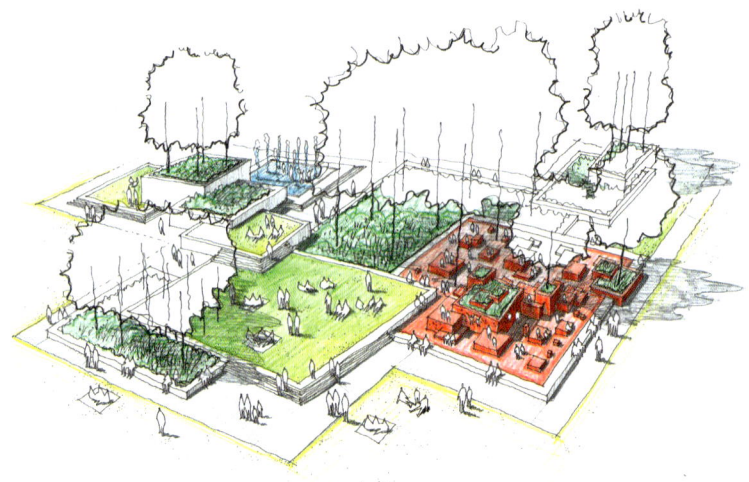
Sketch of Central Garden

Full Site Plan Design

The Residential Zone in the south holds small garden rooms, semi enclosed by tall hedges or feature walls as intimate landscapes for meditation, play areas for children with unique play elements to cater for all age groups, a fitness area, gardens with water features and variety of seating elements positioned in sun and shade. Each uniquely designed room celebrates a moment in life. Surrounding the site, a fitness path is also provided as a sports and recreational trail.

Opposite top: Vehicle entryzone.
Opposite bottom: Edge where vehicles and garden are woven together through the strip logic.

Demonstration Garden Plan

Top: View from above shows the integration of paving, planting, and furniture with the dominant logic of the strip.
Opposite top: Custom seating and lighting appear to be extruded from the paving materials.

Above and right: Planting, wood paving, and planting carefully integrated in the overall patterning strategy.

Opposite: Wavy strips offer playful counterpoint within the overall motif.

Top and bottom: 'Tron' hi-tech entry gateway and custom lighting features provide a branding experience for the new technology district.

Opposite top: Garden of strips: of paving, strips of plants and of furniture form a cohesive yet varied experience.

Opposite bottom left: Shallow water gardens within the strip logic show off their aquatic plants in nighttime glow.

Opposite bottom right: Flowering and deciduous trees structure the garden in a relaxed away and float within the more rigorous layout of the strip motif.

Footscray Park Memorial Garden

Location: Footscray, Victoria, Australia
Area: 1,000 m²
Completion Date: 2013
Landscape Architect: Fitzgerald Frisby Landscape Architecture
Photography: Andrew Lloyd
Client: Maribyrnong City Council

In the aftermath of two world wars, the Footscray community in Melbourne, Australia, was keen to have those who did not return appropriately remembered. An Avenue of Honour was established along the broad boulevard of Geelong Road in the inner western suburb. The avenue consisted of hundreds of ash trees with plaques installed at their bases in memory of individuals.

Over the next half century, the broad avenue also became a focus for vehicle traffic, resulting in incremental road widening, intersection modifications and other road works. Inevitably, these works resulted in the relocation, removal, or damage to plaques and trees.

This project, initiated by Maribyrnong City Council and designed by Fitzgerald Frisby Landscape Architecture, sought to gather all of the remaining plaques together in a stable and respectful setting. This setting is a garden space within the heritage-listed Footscray Park at the northern end of the original avenue. More than 200 plaques are set into new concrete plinths. The shape of the new plinths allows them to interlock together to form low walls, evoking the idea behind the Avenue of Honour – that the sacrifices represented by the individual plaques together create a strong and lasting legacy.

The project also exposed a section of underlying basalt bedrock in close proximity to the plaques, allowing a visual connection between the geological and historic foundations of the community.

Top: The low walls created by the plinths align exactly with the Avenue of Honour where the plaques were originally located.
Opposite top: The memorial garden created is a place for reflection and remembering.

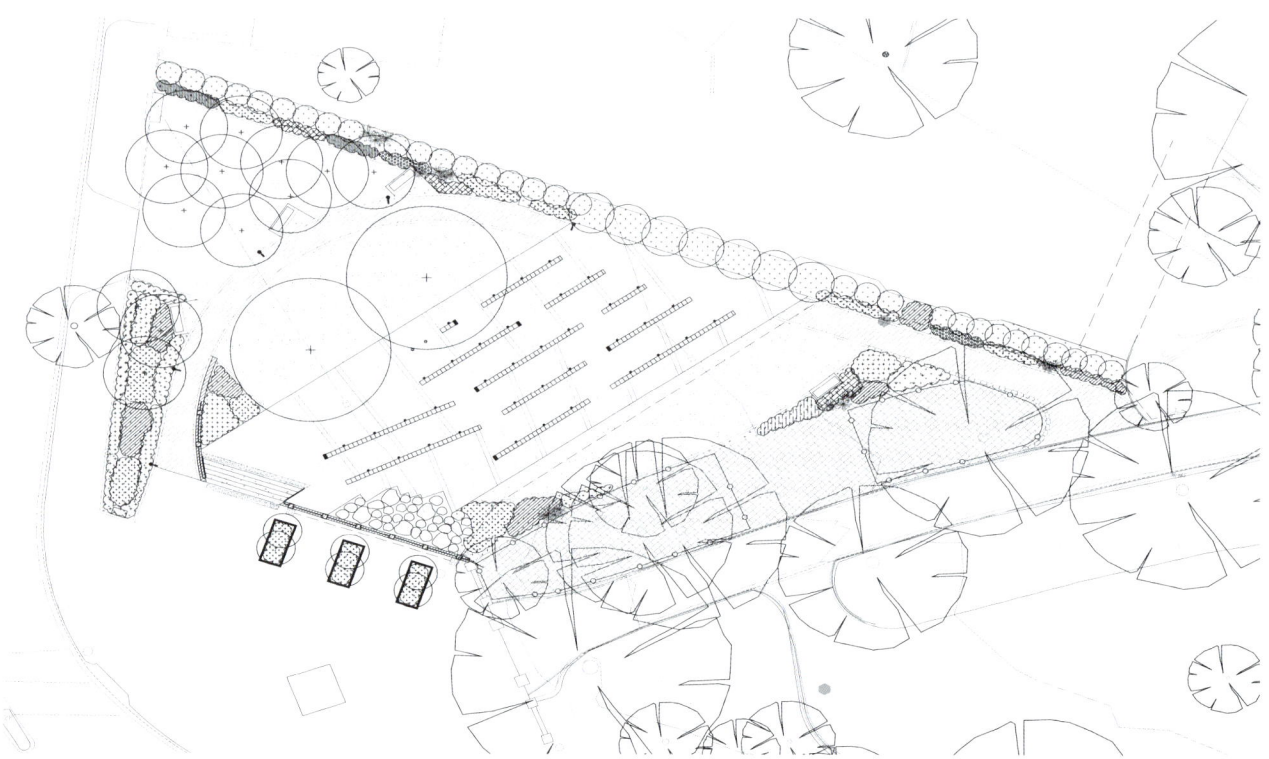

Site Plan

Section A:A scale 1:50 (AI)
1. Steps
2. Retaining wall
3. Existing groundline
4. Precast concrete plinths
5. Existing fence line

A strong connection to the original Avenue of Honour is created by aligning the plinths to exactly match the alignment of the original avenue, including a kink in the road. The original avenue included trees and plaques on both sides of the road as well as within traffic islands separating the main road from the service lanes each side, and the four lines of plinths in the new space reflect this. A fifth line of plinths contains names known to have existed on plaques that have been lost, as well as flag poles used during commemorative ceremonies.

Footscray Park Memorial Garden houses over 200 relocated plaques that commemorate locals who fought in the two world wars.

Fortress Ehrenbreitstein, Coblenz, Germany

Location: Coblence, Germany
Area: 104, 000m²
Completion Date: 2013
Landscape Design: TOPOTEK 1
Client: State of Rhinland-Palatinate, Germany
Photography: Hanns Joosten

At the convergence of the Rhine and Mosel rivers sits the historic Ehrenbreitstein Fortress. This important German national monument was built in the early 19th century on top of a plateau to defend the Rhine Region from French invasion. Today the fortress is preserved as a historic site, with the northern approach serving as a visitors' centre and the historic plateau developed as a museum park. In 2005 a competition was held to develop the park and create additional parking.

The general design concept reorganizes the historic fortress plateau in a dramatic spatial way to improve visitor approach and experience with the historic complex. The car entrance and parking lot are placed at the edge of the plateau, hidden behind a wall of trees. When the fortress was constructed, the immediate landscape was flattened to allow for unimpeded views of the surroundings. The design for the park preserves this artificial topography; the large open plain keeps its monumentality and stages the silhouette of the fortress to the north. Wide, flat circular benches accentuate the vastness of the plane; straight linear paths crisscross the flat plateau, almost like shooting lines, anchoring the empty landscape with an intense rhythmic geometry.

Within the walls of the fortress, an installation piece in the form of a 9m-diameter convex mirror into the ground rests. This mirrored surface reflects the walls and buildings of the fortress, giving the viewer a doubled awareness of the surroundings. A game of perception is created by this installation, essentially an oversized Claude Glass.

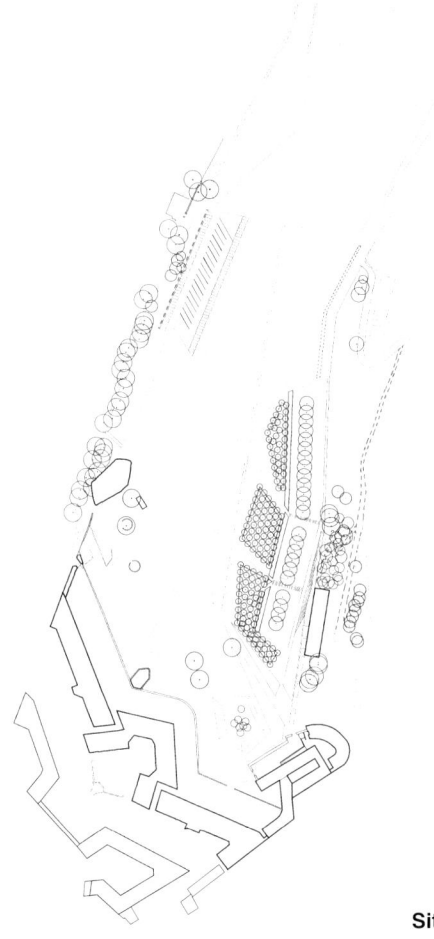

Site Plan

In the 18th and 19th centuries, during the height of picturesque landscape painting, the Claude Glass was a small tinted convex mirror used by picturesque landscape painters to abstract the landscape around them for painting. Painting with the Claude Glass allowed artists to more easily emulate the masters and produce paintings with a tuned colour palette and picturesque framing. Use of the Claude Glass ironically required the painter to sit facing away from the landscape when painting. Today, tourists view the landscape through the lenses of their cameras and smart phones. Their filtered experience of the true landscape is at odds with their attempt to capture it, much like the painters before them. This installation, constructed with reflective aluminum tiles, offers new views of the surrounding fortress, plays with the history of romanticizing the landscape through reflection first with the Claude Glass, and today with digital media.

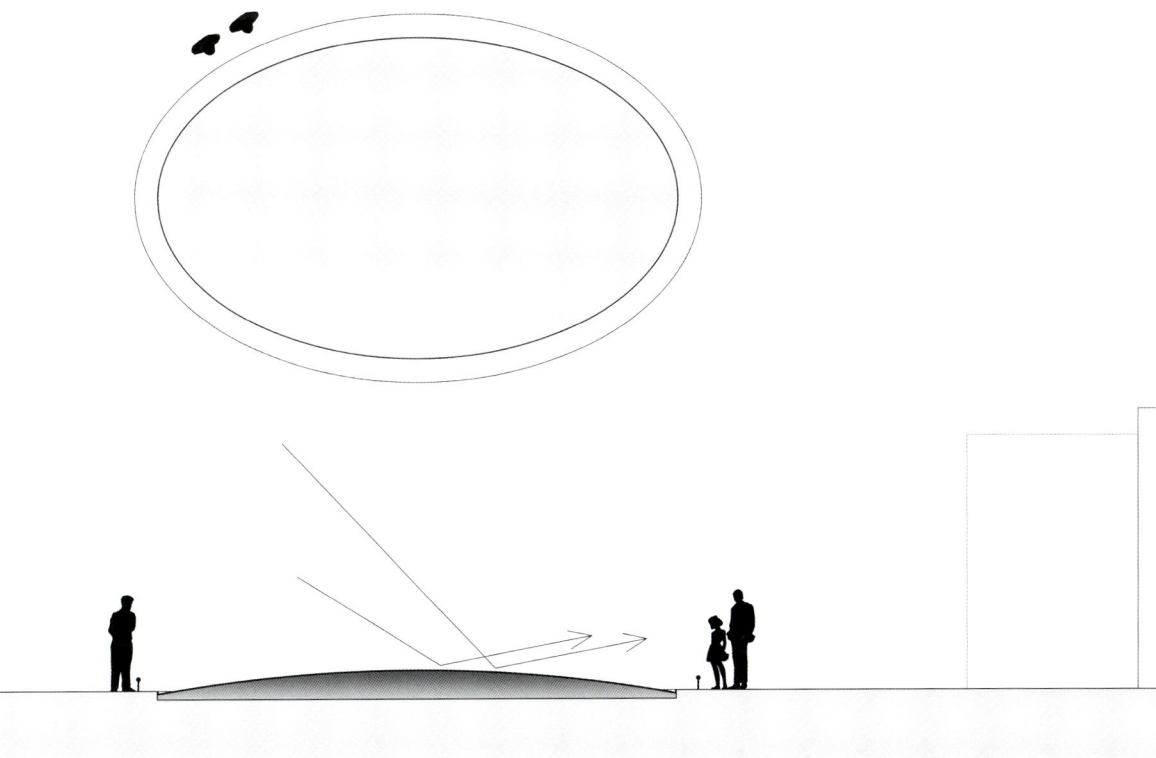

Top: Claude Glass within the walls of the fortress.
Opposite top: Overview of the fortress and Rhine valley.
Opposite bottom: Wall of trees.

Schematic Illustration of Claude Glass

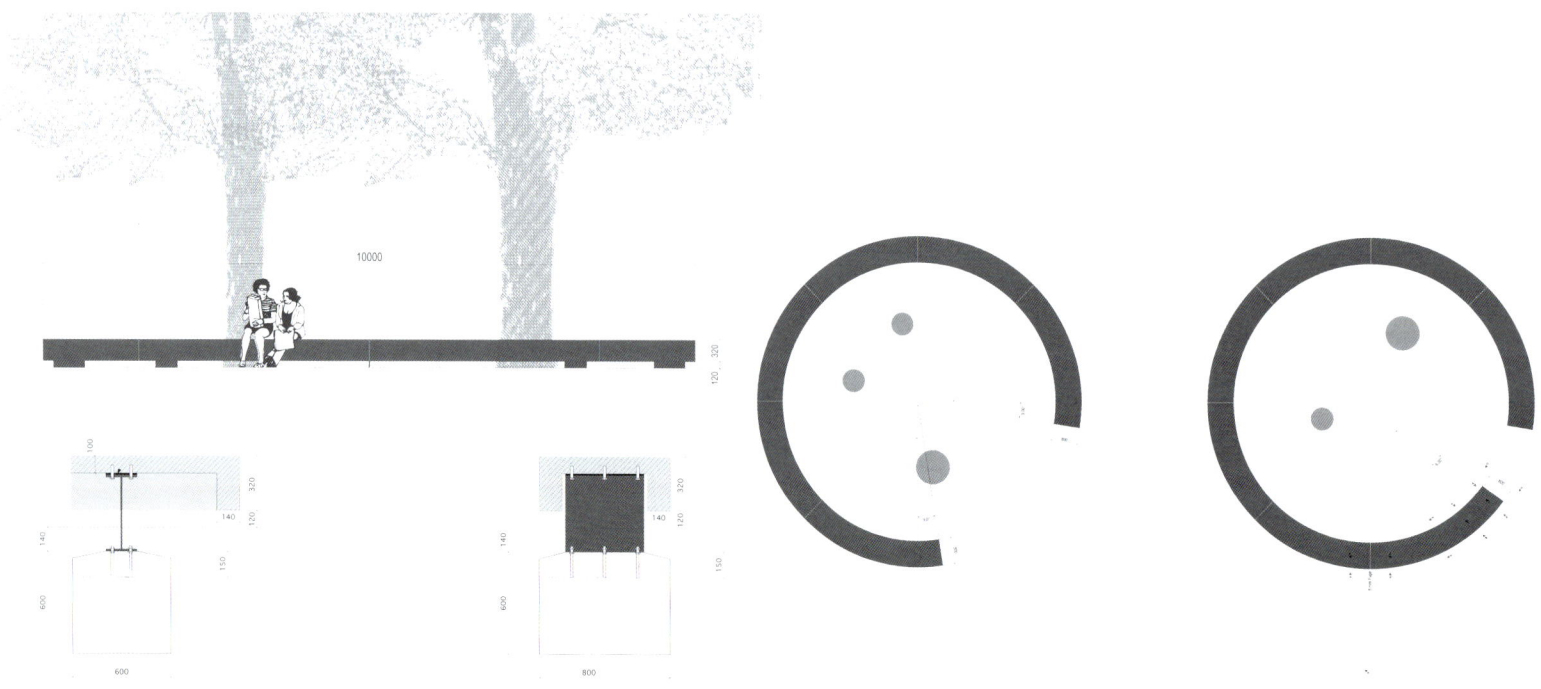

Top: Seating bench on the plateau.
Opposite top: Large horse chestnuts on the wide grassy plateau.
Opposite bottom: Straight linear paths crisscrossing the flat plateau.

Detailed Drawings of The Circular Benches

Sishane Park

Location: Sishane, Beyoglu-Istanbul, Turkey
Area: 32,000m²
Completion Date: 2014
Landscape Design: Arzu Nuhoglu Peyzaj Tasarim
Photography: Olivve.com
Client: Istanbul BuyUnited Kingdomsehir Belediyesi ve Karakoy Gayrimenkul Yatirimlari // Istanbul Greater Municipality and Karaköy Real Estate Development PPP

Sishane Park is a bold shift regarding the public spaces in the center of Istanbul. Located between the southwestern edge of Beyoglu and Tarlabasi Road, the site used to be a park with a fire station that was connected to the water front before a road with a heavy traffic was built in the 1970s. The park penetrates into the streets of the city with an alternative approach and unconventional elements considering the other parks in Istanbul. It is defined by three main features: the silhouette walk, the decks, and the outdoor room. These elements are framed by a rich landscape of various species unique to the Halic in order to enhance the feeling of delight and comfort. It is intended to have deep site lines, be attractive for quality social life and make people touch natural materials including wood rails to lean on and orient one's self within a complex city. There are unique places and experiences waiting people of all ages to discover in Sishane Park.

Animating the public space, Sishane Park has a multi-modal service both to the public and private transportation of Istanbul. Directly connected to the Sishane Metro, it links the pedestrians to the bus/dolmus hubs and Kasimpasa while the 1,000 capacity car park solves the parking problem.

The design team's aim is that Sishane Park forms a gateway to Galata and to the other districts of Beyoglu as well as a link to the social life of Kasimpasa. It is envisioned as a place to experience

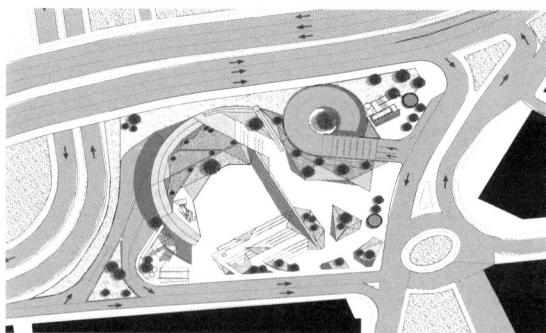

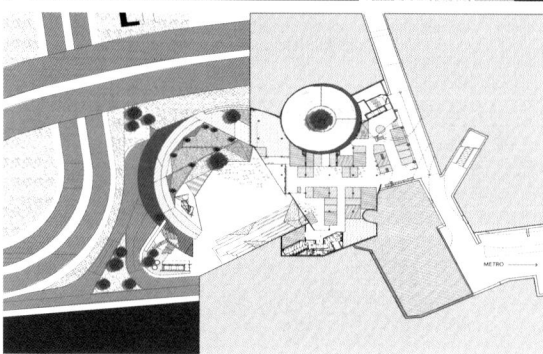

Principal Architect: SANALarc (Alexis Sanal, Murat Sanal)
Project Architects: Begum Öner, Orkun Beydagi, Cibeles Sanchez Llupart,
Project Team: Merve Akdag Öner, Hazar Arasan, Leo Pollock, Cristina Aleman Serrano

Plan of the Silhouette Walk

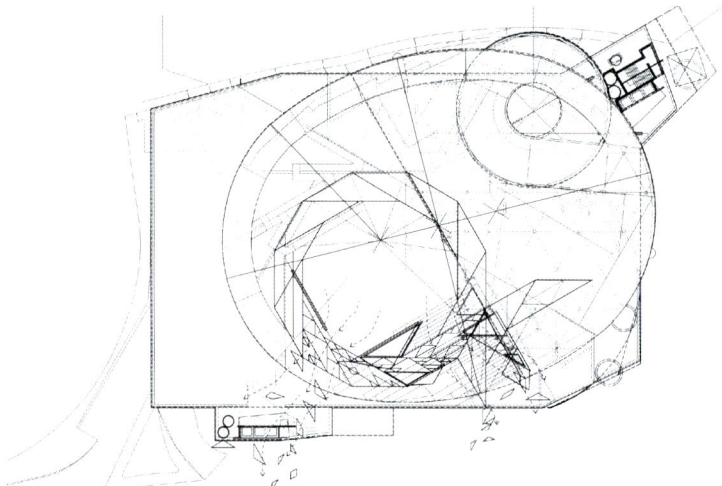

Elevation Through Subway Entrance

the spontaneous urban life of Galata and has a strong connection with the rich natural environment around while offering a new formal and informal platform for cultural venues to program and engage the public in public space.

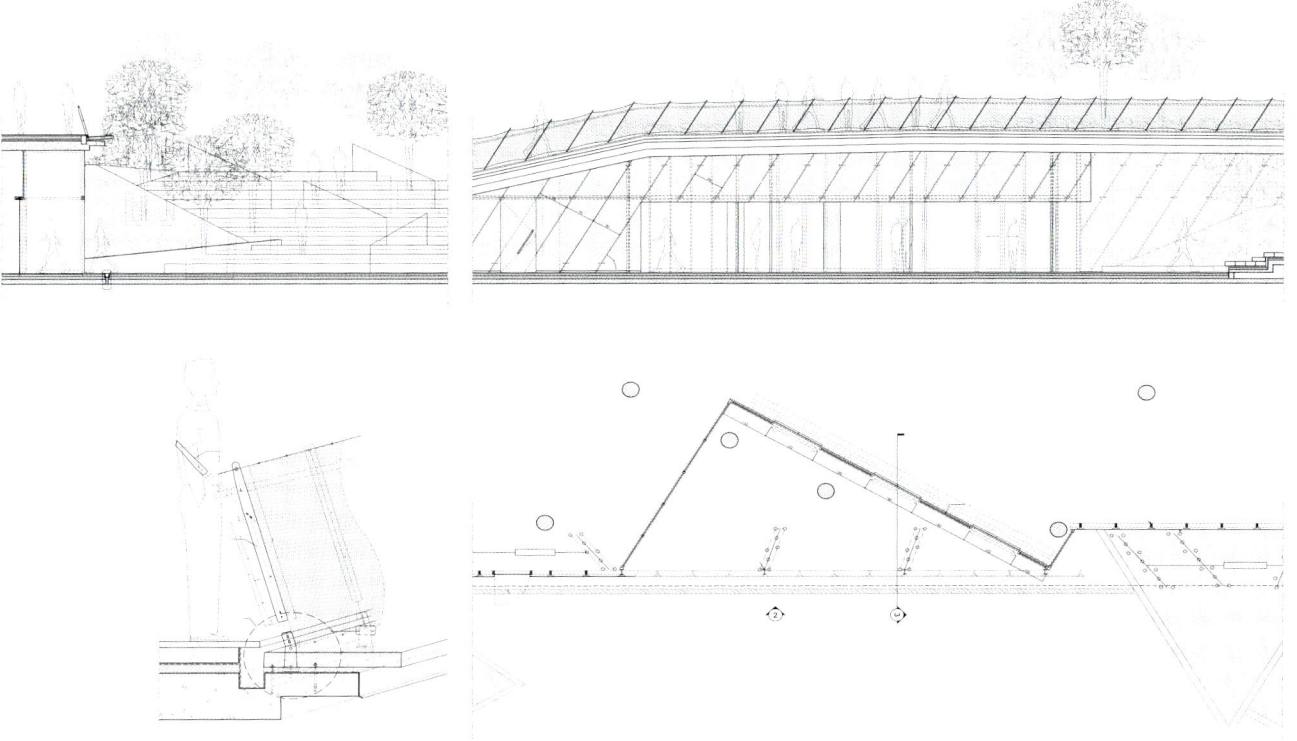

Above: The panorama image of Sishane Park.
Opposite top: The aerial view image of Sishane Park from a distance.

Silhouette Walk

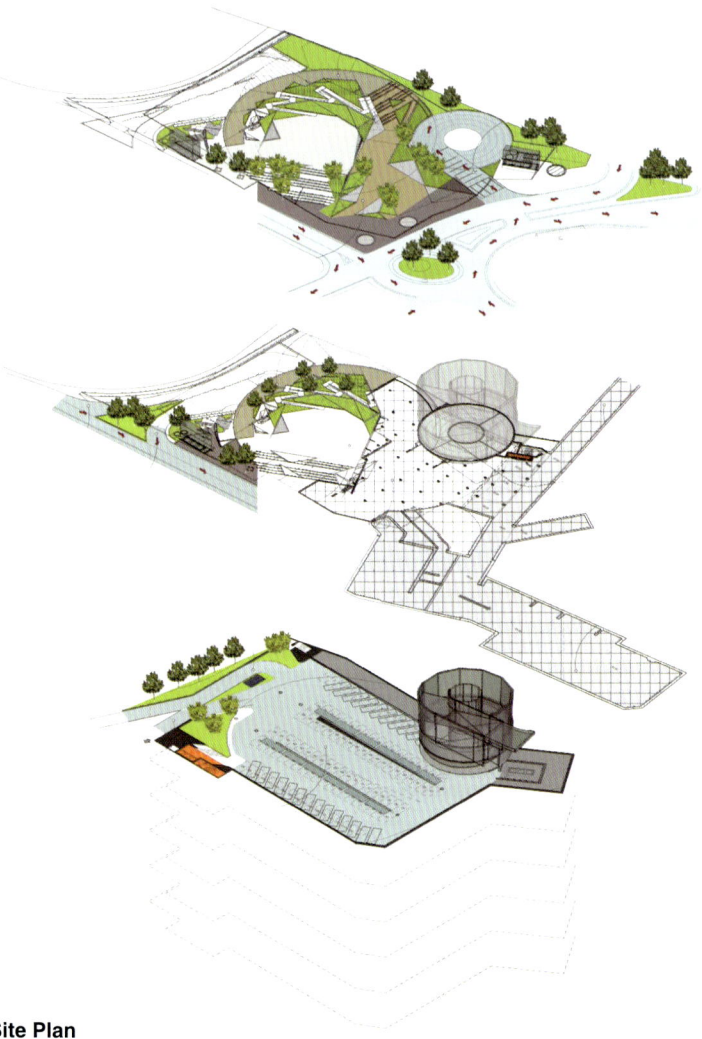

Site Plan

Top: The wooden road at the edge of the fence around Sishane Park.
Opposite top: The central paving area in the middle of the park.
Opposite bottom: The central activity area of Sishane Park.

71

Top: The playground in the sunshine.
Opposite top: The steel fence around Sishane Park.
Opposite bottom: The tree and other green plants between park and the underground parking lot increased the vitality of the parking area.

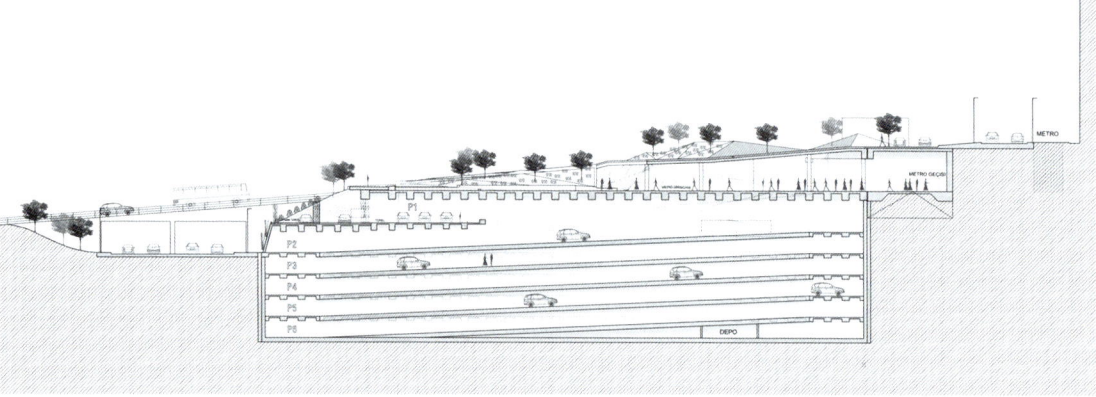

Longitudinal Section

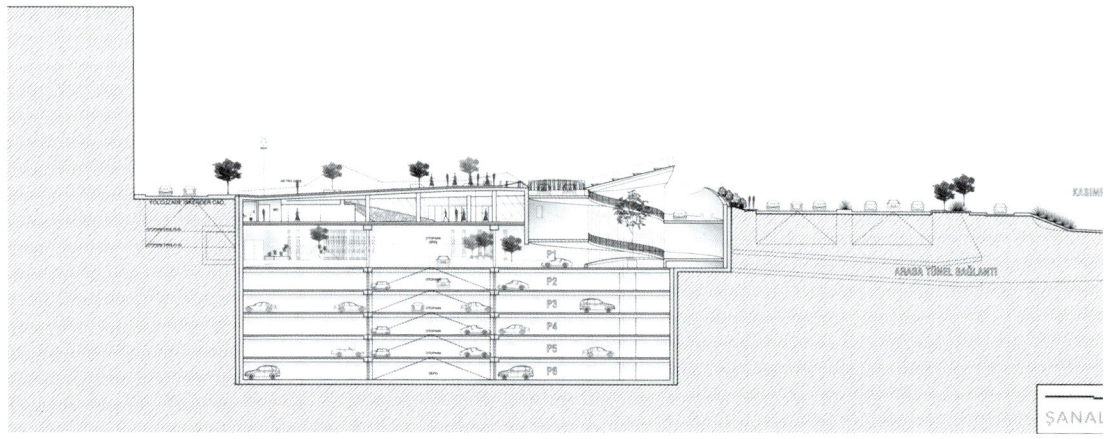

Section

Ulus Savoy Housing

Location: Ulus, Beşiktaş, İstanbul, Turkey
Area: 35,000 m²
Completion Date: 2013
Landscape Design: DS Architecture – Landscape
Photography: Cemal Emden
Client: Çarmıklı Saruhan Partnership

Ulus Savoy Housing, which is located near to the Istanbul Bosphorus region, beside the dynamic structure of the topography, acquires the chance to have excellent Bosphorus views. It rests on a total area of approximately 60,000m² and 35,000m² of it is designed as open spaces. Ulus Savoy is a multi-housing project with 26 blocks settled on a garage structure which is the substructure of the new landscape topography as well. By means of sharp and hard parts, the amorphous structure of the garage is used to embody the landscape. While some parts of the shell are covered with vegetation, other parts are paved with natural stone. On the other hand, this shell works as the backdrop for all of the connection axes and recreational activities. In other words, the constructed topography of the settlement shapes the landscape / garden features of the common spaces. Throughout the project, flat areas serve as the private gardens and the recess areas host the social facilities. Providing a promenade to stroll around the gardens, the partially elevated path plays a great role in the perception of the fractured surfaces of the site.

The steep fragments of the fractured surfaces which are covered by natural stone with particular details become the background of the circular skylights that provide dramatic lighting effects for the garage underneath. As a result of the seasonal changes, throughout the plantation design, dramatic oppositions create dynamic snapshots.

Different levels of shell form the landscape.

Section Plan
1. Green area
2. Underground carpark
3. Sloped paving
4. Service road
5. Social centre

With the exceptionally rich potential of the architectural structure in terms of utilization of wood and stone as the primary materials, the project might be considered as a new interpretation of the nature itself. Introduced as a new version of Bosphorus hillside topography, the vegetation on the fractured surfaces is maintained only by special infrastructural details. Referring to the Bosphorus flora, the newly interpreted maquis group becomes a part of this particular environment.

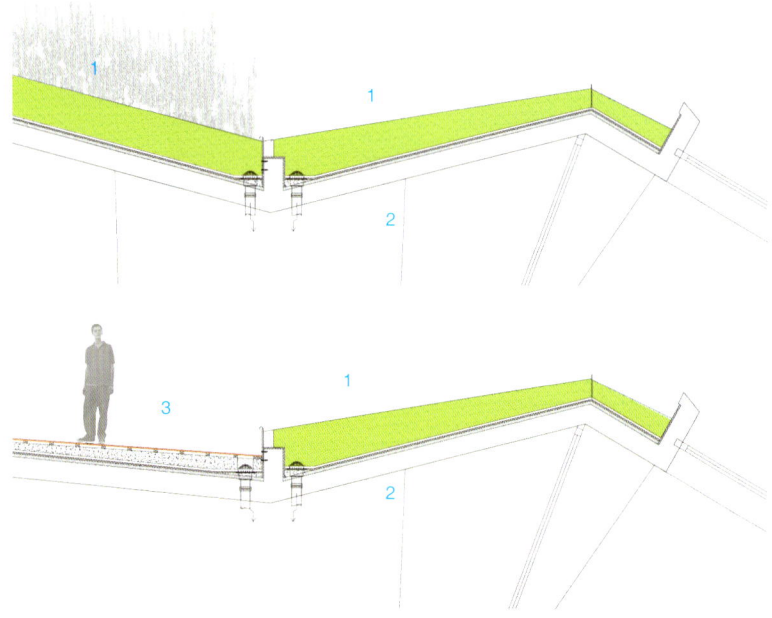
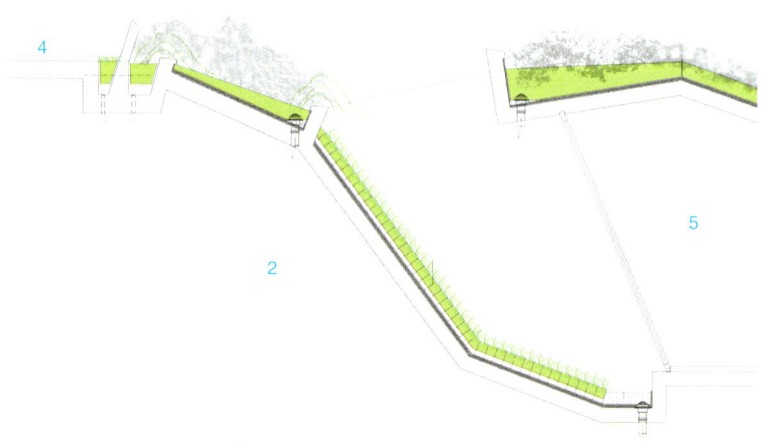

Ulus Savoy Housing Site Plan

1. Entrance (ramp and stairs)
2. Underground car park entrance
3. Social center (swimming pool) and sunbathing wooden deck
4. Children's playground
5. Walking path
6. Park and walking paths

1. Private Gardens

[Trees]
Betula Alba Pendula
Ginkgo Biloba
Hibiscus Syracus
Lagerstromia Japonicum

[Shrubs]
Photinia x Fraserii "Red Robin"

[Perennials]
Phormium Tena "Variegata"

2. Extensive Roof Plants

[Groundcovers]
+ Sedum Mix

3. Common Use Areas

[Trees]
Acer Palmatum "Crimson King"
Bambusa Aurea
Betula Alba Pendula
Cedrus Deodore Aurea
Celtis Australis
Fraxinus Excelsior
Ginkgo Biloba
Magnolia Grandiflora
Pawlonia Tomentosa
Prunus Cerasifera Nigra

[Shrubs]
Caryopteris x Clandonensis
Ceanothus "Blue Pasific"
Coreopsis Grandiflora
Kniphofia Uvaria
Nandina Domestica "Fire Power"
Salvia Officinalis Purpurascens
Santolina Chamaecyparissus
Salvia Purpurea
Teucrium Fruicans

[Perennials]
Carex Elata "Aurea"
Centranthus Ruber
Festuca Glauca

[Climbers]
Amphelopsis Quinquefolia
Bignonia Radicans
Passiflora Caerulea
Wisteria Sinensis

The amorphous structure of the garage (the shell) is used to form the landscape with all its hardness and sharpness parts.

1. Water reservoir
2. Office
3. Corridor
4. Caféteria
5. Lounge
6. Entrance
7. Car park
8. Ramp

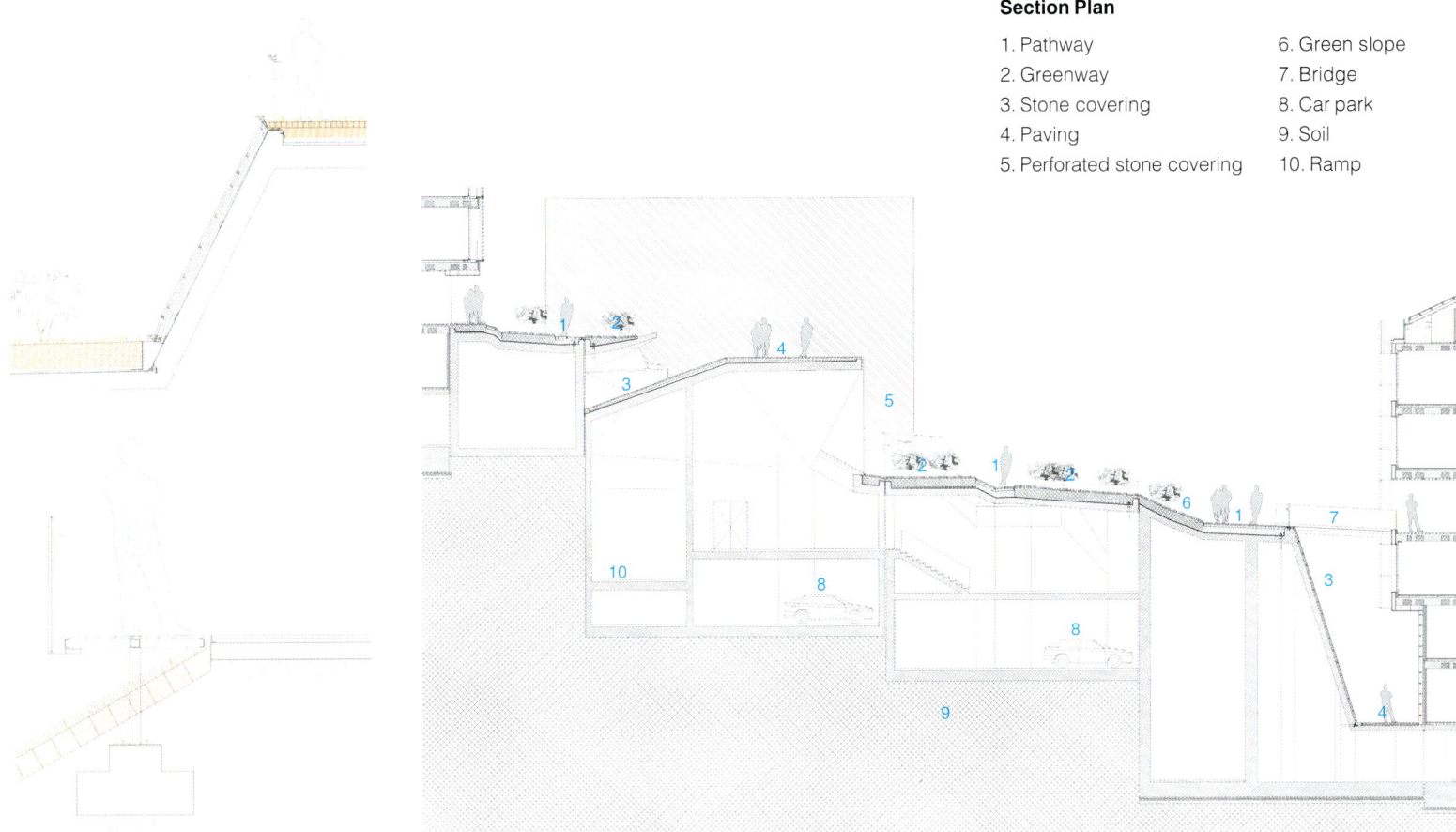

Section Plan

1. Pathway
2. Greenway
3. Stone covering
4. Paving
5. Perforated stone covering
6. Green slope
7. Bridge
8. Car park
9. Soil
10. Ramp

Zelaieta Park

Location: Bizkaia, Spain
Area: 16,000 m²
Completion Date: 2012
Landscape Architect: G&C Arquitectos
Photography: G&C Arquitectos
Client: Municipality of Amorebieta-Etxano

Amorebieta is a medium-sized town in Vizcaya with a practically non-existent historical centre. In the 1970s it suffered from aggressive development, giving priority to the use of vehicles over pedestrians. The need to change this situation consists of increasing the area designated for pedestrians, eliminating street level parking and building an underground parking lot in one of the few possible areas available under the Zelaieta Park. At the same time the opportunity will be taken to renovate the park and its environs.

The Zelaieta Park used to be a private garden so it was designed in accordance with its owners' desires. Through the years several details have been added; a music gazebo, sculptures, and a pond. These things have been constructed haphazardly, not taking into consideration the overall aesthetics of the park, causing it to lose its full potential.

In 2005 the Amorebieta-Etxano town council announced a contest consisting of the renovation of Zelaieta Park and its environs, in order to expand and improve the pedestrian areas, especially those located in the town center. The new public area should be a gathering place designed to attract the citizens of the community. The main idea is to create a logical area with the space available, bringing together the gazebo, playground, promenades, etc., while maintaining the existing trees in the northern area of the park which is comprised of numerous examples of enormous Tilo trees.

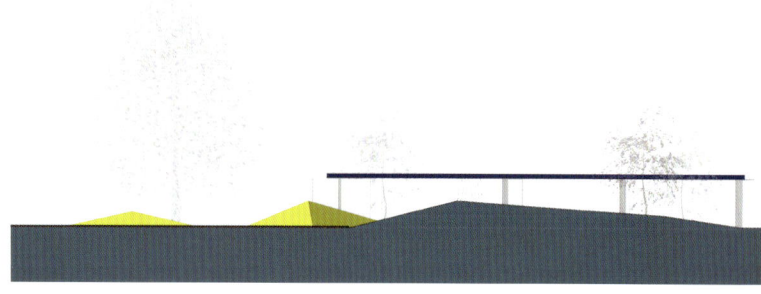
Section 1

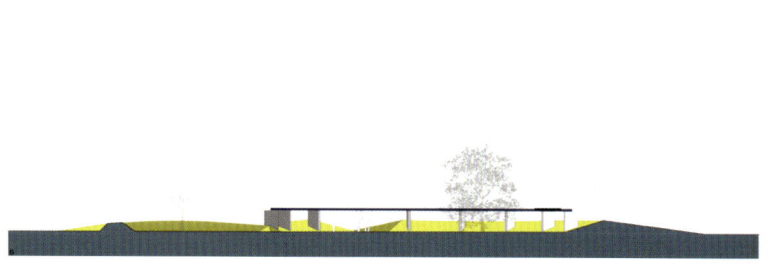
Section 2

The new design has expanded and optimized the uses of the park. It gives service to a wide range of ages and is a focal point of community and social activities. The internal trajectories have been rationalized so that a large number of people can use it daily. Now more aesthetically pleasing, it has generated a positive response and ambience in the community.

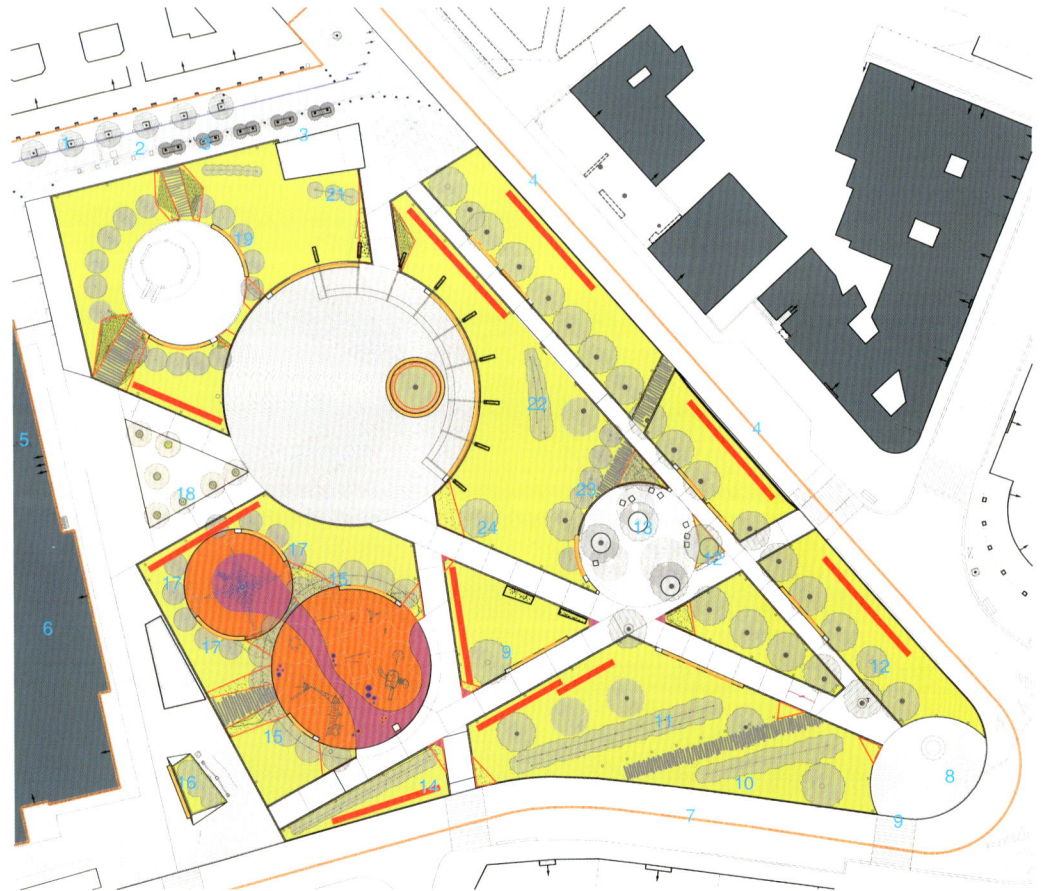

1. Prunus cerasifera pisardi
2. Txiki otaegi street
3. Pyrus caleriana
4. San pedro street
5. Sanitary complex
6. Zelaieta social centre
7. Gudari street
8. Urgozo fountain
9. Magnolia grandiflora
10. Carpinus betulus
11. Acer rubrum
12. Tilia tomentosa
13. Fagus sylvatica
14. Cercis siliquastrum
15. Morus kagamayae
16. Liquidambar
17. Arbutus unedo
18. Malus pendula
19. Prunus pisardii
20. Acer palmatun
21. Gingko
22. Lagerstroemia indica
23. Acer rubrum
24. Magnolia agnolia grandiflora

Section

Elevation

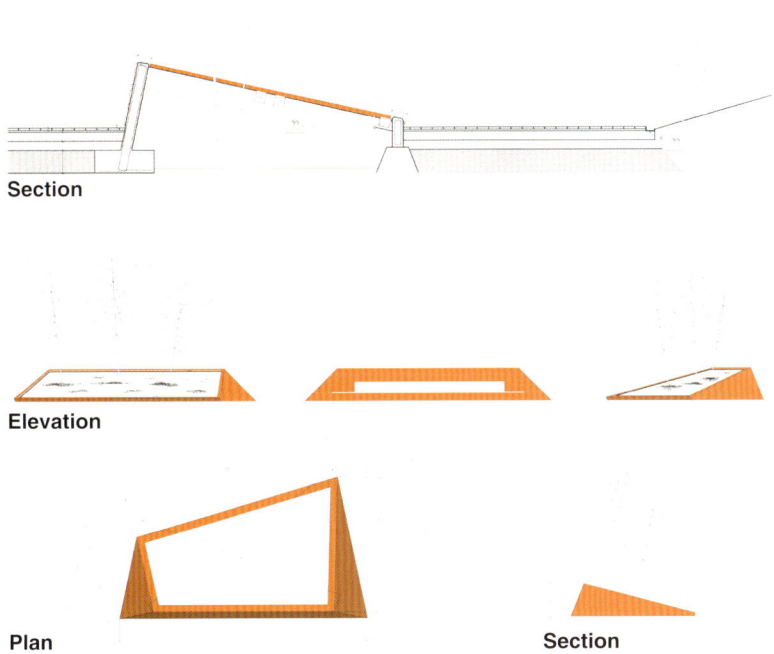

Plan

Section

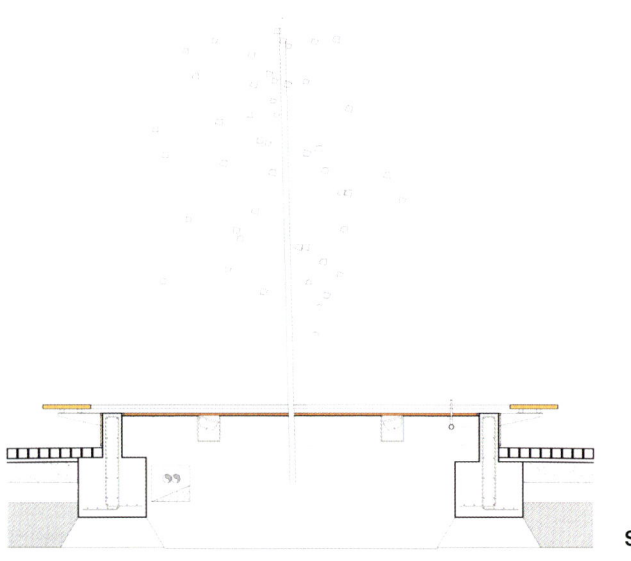

Section

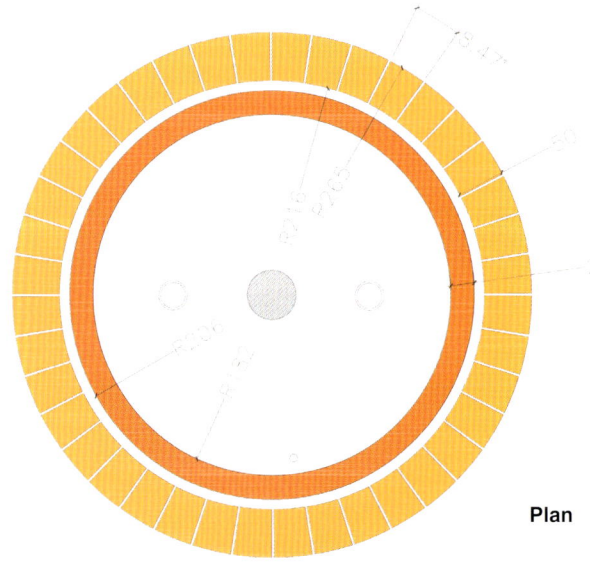

Plan

Top: The wooden chairs along the road and in the square center.
Opposite: The street lamps in the unique form.

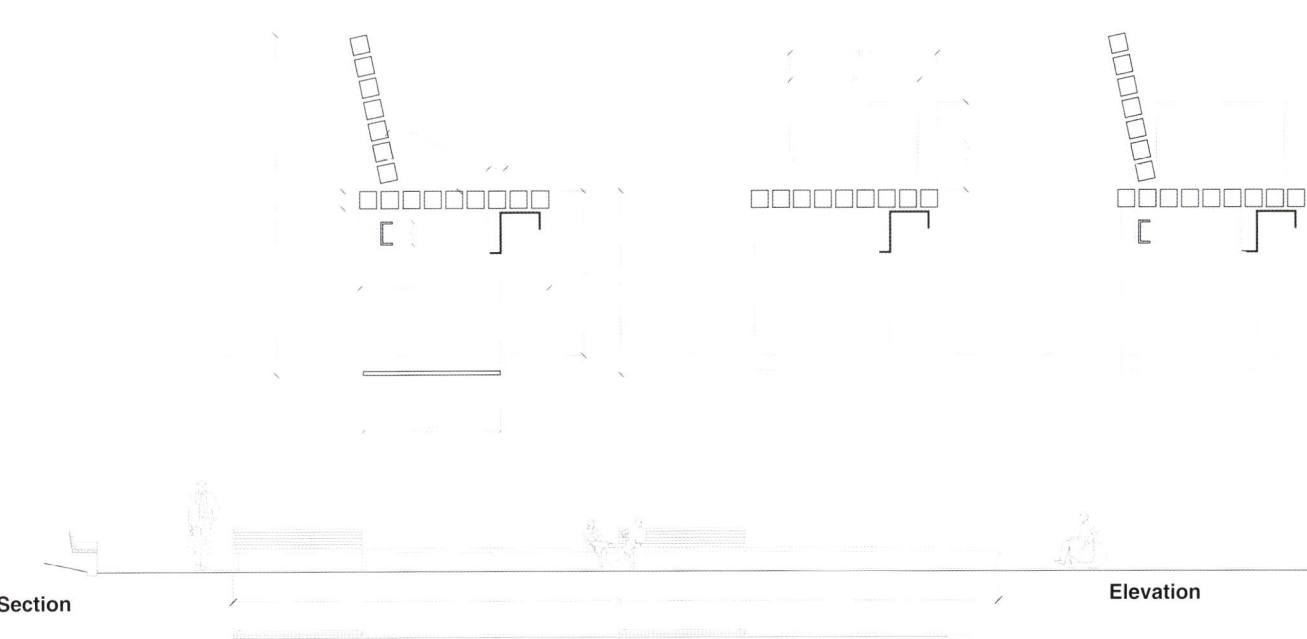

Section Elevation

Plan

Bench Topaketa

Above: Detail images of the road pavement.
Opposite bottom: The drainage service.

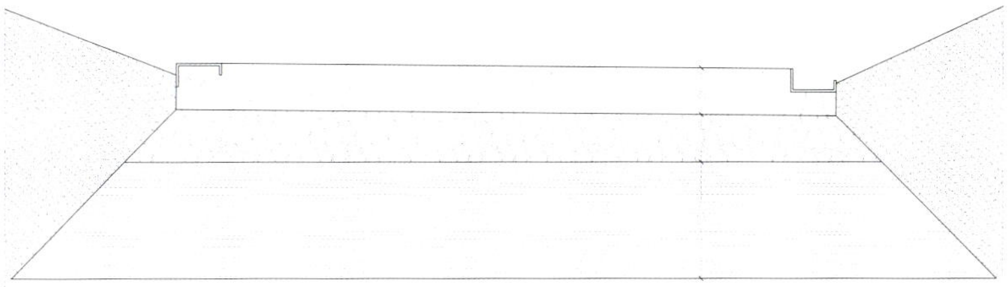

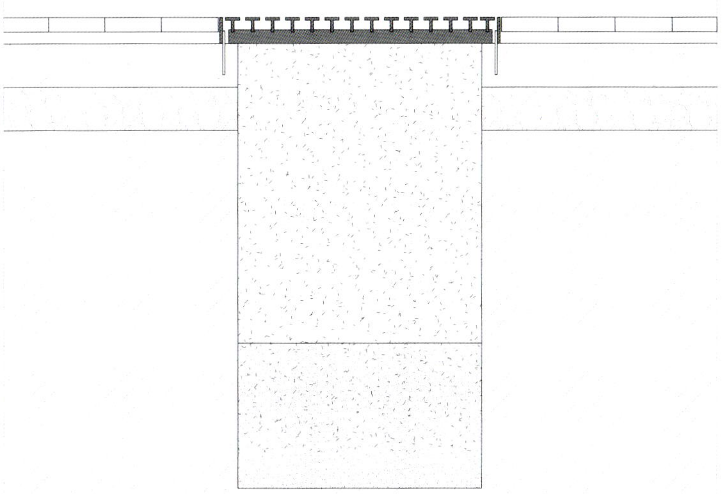

Tree Grid

Sarona Urban Park

Location: Tel-Aviv, Israel
Area: 46,000m²
Completion Date: 2014
Landscape Design: Dan Zur-Lior Wolf Landscape Architects Ltd.
Photography: Amit Hass and Zur Wolf
Client: The Israel Land Administration

"Sarona" Park is an urban complex of recreation and entertainment that stretches over 45 dunam in the heart of Tel-Aviv. The park was designed with the historic buildings of the German Protestant settlers who established it in 1871. The new design revives the old spirit of the settlement as an urban complex of recreation and entertainment, without abandoning the settlements landscape and agriculture indicators.

The park pathways recreate the privet farm plots around each house, where garden and useful plants were grown. The main streets in the renewed settlement are paved for pedestrian use and are defined by low fences separating the home plots from the street, much like the old street section.

The planning process included a thorough survey for the hundreds of existing trees and a conservation survey for each of the 36 remaining historic buildings, some of which had to be moved backwards from the expanding Kaplan Street route, in a remarkable engineering effort.

The park is divided into four quarters and one more part comprising the historic winery and distillery. Each part was analyzed to characterize its appropriate modern uses. The main gathering area is placed where the school and the old settlements hall used to be, an ecological pond replaces the old water retaining pool, a dancing and skating arena is placed where the settlement tennis courts used to be, a plants nursery is planned where the old nursery used to stand, and the olive press will be diverted into a museum on olive oil production.

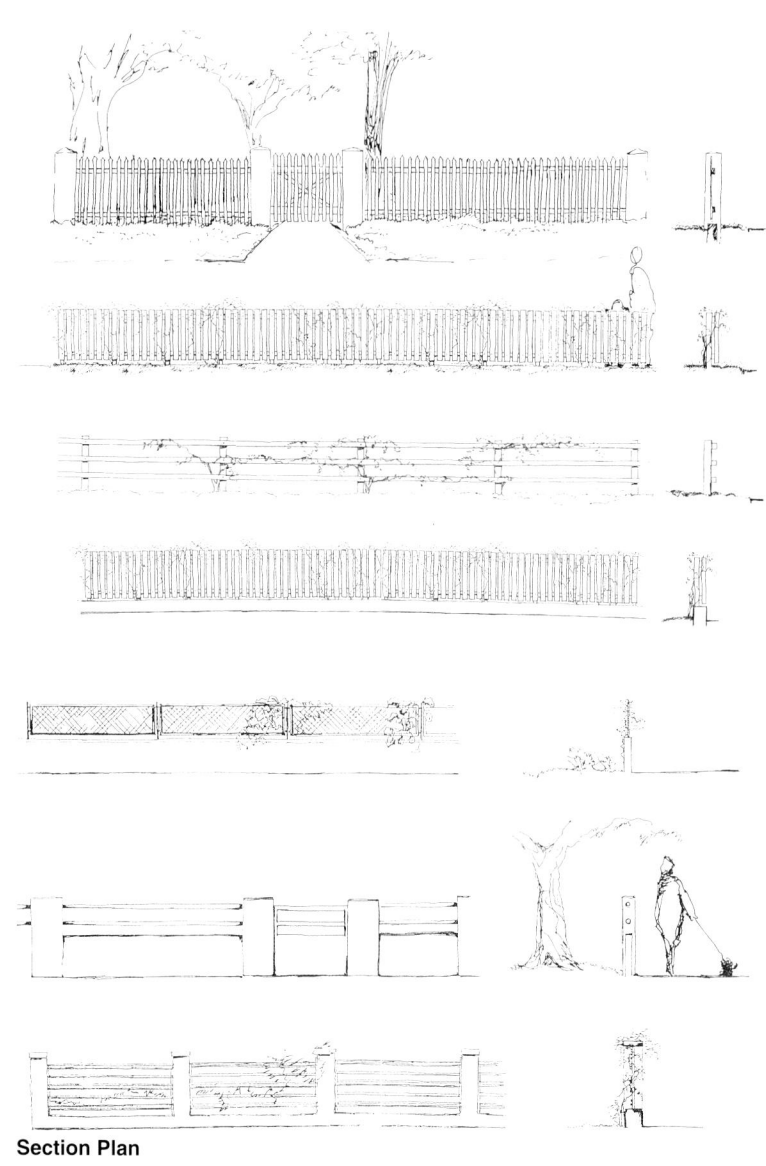

Section Plan

The music garden for small events and gatherings, in which exists a "storage pool" in the form of a biological water pool, is an additional reference to the flowing water technology as shown at the main square. The music concept refers to the developed social life of the templers, which included various musical ensembles.

Plan
1. Kaplan Street
2. Arania Street
3. Music garden
4. Skating ring
5. Albert Mendler Street
6. Visitor center
7. Central square
8. David Elazae Street
9. Nursery
10. Goverment building
11. David Elazar Street
12. Kalman Magen Street
13. The winery
14. Winery square
15. Vineyard
16. The distillery
17. Menachem Begin Road

An historic narrow street, defined on either side by citrus trees, refers to the templers, citrus industry.

A sketch shows the cross sectional design concept for the historical streets in the park. Street cross section showing an atmosphere of agricultural settlement with fences and beds assigned on the front, quite similar to the historic street section.

The skating rink and dance square, in the place of the old colony's tennis courts, are paved with a cast of terrazzo patterned enlargement of an existing paved surface inside one of the buildings. The square is designed for the use of large scale public events as well as for dancing events and skating.

An historic street defined either side by low walls. These are built in blocks drawn from the templers, buildings coverings. The blocks have been designed and manufactured specifically for the project.

The main square of the park is located at the colony's public space. The design of the square refers to the flowing water technology the templers first used in Israel: a wind pump that "streams the water to the reservoir" which is now designed as a biological water pool.

Chapter 2 Public Plaza Design

A public plaza is a community amenity that serves a variety of users including building tenants and visitors and members of the public. This space type may function as pedestrian site arrival points, homes for public art, settings for recreation and relaxation, and inconspicuous security features for high-profile buildings.

Plazas are a beneficial feature of any lively streetscape. Programmatically, plazas are strongly linked to the lobby space type. Both are a "public face" for a building that welcomes and orients visitors.

1. Design Principles of Public Plaza Design

Every successful public space must respond to: its physical environment – nearby buildings and uses; its local climate – sun, wind, rain and so on; its own history; its users. It must include some attractive elements for people – safety, beauty, activity, and focal point(s).

1.1 History, Tradition, and Character

The design of the specific forms and patterns has through time and space, to form a common human appeal, they also form the traditional classical design. The form of the town square is a significant historical artifact. The pattern and interaction of multiple strong geometrical elements – squares, circles, diagonals – traditionally forms the structure and foundation for important civic spaces. Different parts of the use of spaces, according to different focus on the visual and physical manufacturing of feelings, is another kind of universal design principle.

In an existing, historical civic space, it is important to respect the essential elements of the historical form and order while updating the elements to make them relevant to the present and future (just as their original, historical founders did at their creation). Design elements should be injected with local flavor and character, such as local scenery, local industry, local history, and existing arts and crafts.

1.2 Activity and Sociability

A public plaza creates a wide range of use, both formal and informal: it provides a large number of seats – some that can be in the sun, some that can be in the shade; it provides a comfortable environment and activity facilities which can attract people – young to old, singles, families or groups; public plaza provides a comfortable environment and proper facilities to make people have reasons to stay in different times – passing through, meeting up or taking a break during work or school hours, socializing or enjoying events and entertainment during off hours, evenings and weekends; it also offers many choices – for solitude or for gathering, for relaxing or for watching or participating, choices to be in the open or to be in a secluded area (to view or to be in view).

1.3 Comfort and Appearance

Access and linkages are essential to the success of a public space. Square surroundings shall provide convenience and safety of inlet and outlet. The function and appearance of a public plaza are closely linked, but are not identical, as in a home's living room. Therefore, to create a perfect integral design, every detail should be measured in terms of function and appearance.

Successful public spaces can present grace and visual appeal, in order to attract the public. The choice of building materials should also reflect a certain quality and durability.

Even if all of the other elements of a successful public space are present, without the look and feel of safety and cleanliness, a place will fail or fall far short of its potential. The space must be wel-maintained and cared-for, with a maintenance plan that is realistic and sustainable. There must be an obvious sense of continuous informal surveillance from a critical mass of users and from the surroundings, and regular law enforcement should be used to minimize anti-social behaviour .

2. Public Plaza Design Standards

2.1 Dimensions

To ensure spaces of adequate size for the public and accommodate the required amenities, the minimum area for public plazas is 2,000 square feet. This minimum size is adequate for small, vest-pocket parks and can comfortably accommodate seating, planting, and other required amenities. The 2009 text amendment revised the regulations regarding open areas that are not designated as public plaza (non-bonused open areas). Non-bonused open areas that are located adjacent to a public plaza and a sidewalk would no longer require a buffer, thus permitting greater pedestrian circulation along the street line.

2.2 Configuration

Public plazas should generally be regular in shape (i.e., rectangular, square, etc). However, to allow articulation of building façades facing onto plaza and flexibility in landscape design, the plaza regulations allow for small areas of the plaza to take the form of alcoves or niches adjacent to the main portion of the plaza. If so designed, the main portion of the plaza is termed the "major portion" of the public plaza and must account for at least 75% of the plaza area. The smaller areas are then considered to be "minor portions" and are limited to no more than 25% of the plaza area. Major and minor portions of the public plaza are generally held to the same design standards, although major portions are required to meet stricter requirements related to dimensions and visibility. Major portions of public plazas are required to have average width and depth of 40 feet. To allow for additional flexibility in the configuration and design of the public plaza, up to 20% of the plaza area may be less than 40 feet in depth.

2.3 Locational Restrictions

To ensure continuity of building street walls, public plazas may not be located within 175 feet of other plazas or parks. For new public plazas that are proposed to be located across the street from an existing public open area, a waiver of the locational restrictions would be allowed by the Chairperson during certification if the Chairperson finds that such proposed location would facilitate and contribute toward greater pedestrian circulation between the proposed space and an existing public open area. This portion of the 2007 text was amended in 2009 in order to clarify its intent- that the 175 feet is measured along the street line.

2.4 Restrictions on Orientation

South-facing plazas are generally preferred, unless particular lot configurations prevent such orientation. Where lots do not have south-facing portions or where the south-facing portions are less than 40 feet in width, the plaza is permitted to face either east or west. In no cases are plazas permitted to be only north-facing.

To ensure that developments can comply with mandatory street wall regulations found in certain zoning districts and to maximize light and air to public plazas, a waiver of public plaza orientation regulations is available at the time of certification if the Chairperson finds that the orientation regulations conflict with mandatory street wall regulations and that a better light condition would result from such modification.

2.5 Visibility

Visibility into and throughout the public plaza is of paramount importance in promoting a sense of openness and safety. Consequently, public plazas are required to be completely visible when viewed from any adjacent street frontage. However, to maintain design flexibility for certain public plazas that are located on corners where streets do not meet at 90 degree angles, the visibility requirements only require complete visibility from one street frontage and at least 50% visibility from the other street frontage.

2.6 Minor Portions

As described above, the regulations permit variation from standards related to dimensions and visibility for up to 25% of the public plaza area, referred to as the minor portion of the public plaza. Such minor portions provide additional flexibility in building and plaza design, such as chamfered corners and small recesses, which enhances the attractiveness, openness, and variation of public plazas. Minor portions are permitted to be smaller and less fully visible than the major portion of the public plaza, provided that the minor portions are directly adjacent to the major portion, are not less than 15 feet in width and depth, and are fully visible when viewed from the major portion. To ensure that minor portions not located on the street frontage are well integrated with the major portion and provide valuable additional plaza area, such areas are required to have a width to depth ratio of at least 3:1 and to have their longest dimension oriented along the edge of the major portion.

2.7 Regulations for Through Block Public Plazas

Through block public plazas are those spaces located on the midblock that connect two street frontages. Such public plazas are required to contain at least one circulation path at least 10 feet in width connecting the two streets. The circulation path need not be straight and may contain amenities such as trees planted flush-to-grade and light stanchions. In addition, portions of adjoining buildings that front on the public plaza for more than 120 feet are required to be set back from the public plaza at least 10 feet at a height between 60 and 90 feet. This requirement ensures that through block public plazas are not located between inordinately tall sheer building walls and to allow a greater sense of openness and human scale within the space.

2.8 Sidewalk Frontages

Review of existing plazas has demonstrated that plaza usebility is significantly determined by the relationship between the sidewalk and plaza. To facilitate access into public plazas from adjacent streets and to enliven the areas where public plazas meet the sidewalk, there are certain regulations applicable to the area within the first 15 feet of a public plaza called the "sidewalk frontage". The sidewalk frontage of a public plaza is required to have a minimum 50% of its area free of obstructions. In addition, plazas that front on a street intersection are required to maintain a clear area within 15 feet of the intersection. The remaining 50% of the sidewalk frontage may contain obstructions such as fixed and moveable seating, plantings and trees, light stanchions, public space signage, trash receptacles, or other design elements that are permitted within public plazas and are under two feet in height. The 2009 text amendment clarified that the clear, unobstructed area is measured perpendicular to the street line and that other amenities such as planting walls and water features are permitted to be greater than two feet in height, as long as such amenities are within three feet of a plaza wall.

2.9 Elevation

Plazas with dramatic differences in elevation between sidewalks and plazas lessen their usebility, attractiveness, and perception of safety. The regulations now require that public plazas should generally be located at the same level of adjoining sidewalks and streets. Minor changes in elevation, not to exceed two feet above the level of the adjacent sidewalk, are permitted.

To permit additional flexibility in the design of large public plazas, a maximum of 20% of public plazas greater than 10,000 square feet in size, may be permitted to have an elevation up to four feet above the level of the adjacent sidewalk, provided that such elevated area is located more than 25 feet from the sidewalk (street) line. Plazas may generally not be sunken below street level; however plazas fronting on steeply sloping streets – between 2.5% and 5.0% grade change along the length of the plaza – are accorded additional flexibility in accommodating elevation changes and may have an elevation up to one foot below the level of the adjacent sidewalk.

2.10 Steps

Minimum and maximum step dimensions are specified to ensure that changes in elevation are comfortable, safe, and appropriate to a plaza setting. Steps are permitted to have heights between 4 and 6 inches. Step treads are required to be at least 17 inches in width, except that 5 inch steps are permitted to have treads at least 15 inches in width.

2.11 Circulation Paths

To ensure sufficient accessibility into and within public plazas, circulation paths are required that are at least 8 feet in width and extend to at least 80% of the depth of the plaza. Circulation paths are required to connect each of the street frontages on which the plaza fronts as well as all plaza and building entrances and major design features of the public plaza, including seating areas and open air cafés. Trees planted flush-to-grade, light stanchions, public space signage, and trash receptacles are permitted within circulation paths.

2.12 Permitted Obstructions

Public plazas are generally required to be open to the sky and unobstructed, except for certain permitted obstructions such as planting, seating, and other plaza amenities.

(1) Maximum Extent of Obstruction

Plazas less than 10,000 square feet have a maximum obstruction of 40% of the plaza area. Plazas greater than 10,000 square feet have a maximum obstruction limit of 50% of the plaza area. To compensate for café-related amenities such as seating and tables, plazas with permitted open air cafés are allowed an additional 10% of the plaza area in obstructions. While elevated planters are typically considered obstructions for the purpose of calculating the amount of obstructed area in a public plaza, lawns or grassy areas do not count as obstructions, provided that they are intended for public access and do not exceed 6 inches in height above surrounding walking areas.

(2) Canopies, Awnings, and Marquees

Canopies, awnings and marquees associated with building and retail entrances can enhance the use of a public plaza by building tenants and retail customers in inclement weather conditions. However, these obstructions, if not carefully designed, can dramatically impair the sense of openness and public nature of the plaza area. Canopies, marquees, and awnings are limited to a maximum area of 250 square feet and to a maximum 15-foot projection from the building façades. Such canopies are required to be located at least 15 feet above the surface of the plaza and vertical supports are prohibited. However, canopies associated with the entrances to residential buildings are permitted to project further than 15 feet and have vertical supports if the canopy is located entirely within 10 feet of the edge of the plaza. This allows for comfortable automobile drop-offs or taxi pick-ups for residential tenants, for example, without significantly impacting the larger plaza area.

(3) Prohibitions

Certain obstructions are generally prohibited from all public plazas due to their detrimental impact on usebility and enjoyment of the public space. Garage entrances, driveways, parking spaces, loading berths, exhaust vents, mechanical equipment, and building trash storage facilities are prohibited within all public plazas. Any such uses located adjacent to a public plaza are required to be screened or concealed from view. In addition, vents and mechanical equipment are prohibited on any adjacent building walls within 15 feet of the level of the public plaza. Air intake vents and intake shafts, such as those to serve underground facilities, are permitted within public plazas if they are incorporated into plaza design features and do not impair visibility within the plaza.

3. Public Plaza Design Elements

3.1 Seating

The provision of abundant, well-designed, and comfortable seating is one of the most critical elements of public plaza design. Plaza designers should carefully consider the variety, dimensions, location, and configuration of seating with the intent to maximize opportunities for comfortable and convenient seating that emphasizes social interaction.

(1) Variety

There are six types of seating that may be used to satisfy the seating requirements for public plazas: moveable seating, fixed individual seats, fixed benches, seat walls, planter ledges, and seating steps.

All public plazas are required to provide two of these seating types, while plazas between 5,000 and 10,000 square feet are required to provide three types. Plazas greater than 10,000 square feet are required to provide moveable seating as one of the three required seating types.

Social seating – seats that are located in close proximity to one another and in configurations that facilitate social interaction – are a basic seating arrangement that should be provided across all seating types wherever possible. Movable tables and chairs are the most flexible form of social seating, although angled and curved benches and groupings of fixed seats can achieve the same purpose.

A substantial proportion of seats in a plaza should have backs to facilitate comfort and usebility by people of all ages and abilities. To ensure sufficient variety in seating types in the public plaza, seating steps and walls are limited to no more than 15% of the total required seating in the public plaza.

(2) Dimensions

Seating that is too narrow, too high, or too short inhibits the usebility of a space and runs counter to the goal of providing an enjoyable and comfortable space for a variety of users. Seats are required to be at least 18 inches deep and between 16 and 20 inches in height.

To allow for generous plantings, seating provided on planter ledges is required to be at least 22 inches deep. Seating steps can provide flexible seating – from simple perches to generous, amphitheater-style seating – and are permitted to range between six and 20 inches in height.

Seats should generally be between 16 and 20 inches in height and 18 inches in depth. If backs are provided, they should be at least 14 inches high and reclined or contoured for comfort.

(3) Location

Many existing plazas locate seating deep within the plaza area. Such seating can provide a desirable sense of refuge from the city; however, the lack of seating at the plaza entrance often results in a barren condition and an underutilized plaza. To ensure that adequate seating is provided throughout the public plaza, a portion of the required seating in the public plaza must be located within 15 feet of the sidewalk. The minimum amount of seating required in the sidewalk frontage is one linear foot of seating for every two linear feet of public plaza street frontage. To ensure that this seating is comfortable and engages the public by being oriented toward the street, 50% of such seating is required to have backs and 50% of the seats with backs are required to face the sidewalk. The 2009 text amendment enhanced the regulations for seating with backs to require that such seats would not be greater than 20 inches in depth. This revised provision is based upon the body's natural seating posture, thus ensuring that required seating is useble.

(4) Prohibitions

Deterrents to seating, such as spikes, rails, or deliberately uncomfortable materials or shapes, placed on surfaces that would otherwise be suitable for seating are prohibited within public plazas. These types of devices can be seen throughout existing plazas and compromise the useability and public nature of these spaces.

Devices incorporated into seating that are intended to prevent damage caused by skateboards and rollerblades are generally permitted. Such deterrents are required to be spaced at least 5 feet apart from one another, be constructed of high-quality materials that are integrated with the seating design, and should not inhibit seating.

3.2 Planting and Trees

Trees and other planted areas are essential components of successful and enjoyable public spaces. A balance must be struck between abundant, lush, and generous planting and the need for adequate sun and openness in the public plaza. The 2009 text amendment revised the 2007 design regulations to provide a better balance between hard surfaces and planted areas, such as ground-level planting.

(1) Trees

A minimum of four trees are required within every public plaza. For every 1,000 square feet of plaza, four caliper inches of additional trees are required. The use of caliper inches, rather than an absolute number of additional trees, allows for additional flexibility in planting design. The requirement can be met by either providing fewer trees with larger diameter trunks or a greater number of smaller, multi-stemmed species. For example, a 10,000 square foot plaza would be required to provide four trees, plus an additional 40 caliper inches. The additional caliper inches could be provided in ten four-caliper inch trees, eight five-caliper inch trees, or four ten-caliper inch trees.

At least 50% of required trees should be planted flush-to-grade and must be surrounded by a porous surface at least 5 feet in width that allows water to penetrate to the tree roots while at the same time accommodating pedestrian circulation. Trees provided in planting beds are required to have a minimum of 5 feet square of porous area, such as mulch, pebbles, or planted area to allow for water penetration. The 2009 text amendment revised the requirements for tree plantings to allow half of required trees to be planted either flush-to-grade or in at-grade planting beds. The updated provision allows additional design flexibility without encumbering pedestrian circulation.

(2) Additional Plantings

As per the 2007 public plaza regulations, public plazas are required, in addition to the tree requirements described above, to provide at least one additional planted amenity within the public plaza area in the form of additional trees or planted area. To encourage greater landscaping variety and to prevent plazas from being excessively hard-surfaced, the 2009 text amendment simplified and upgraded the plantings regulations to require 20% of the plaza to be covered in ground-level planting. The revised planting requirement could take the form of planting beds, groundcover or accessible lawns. Plantings in hanging containers do not count as required plantings.

(3) Irrigation and Drainage

To ensure that trees and other plants can successfully establish and grow in an urban environment, irrigation is required for all planted areas unless drought-resistant species are specified in the planting plans. Drainage systems are also required in planted areas located above subsurface structures such as garages or cellars.

3.3 Lighting and Electrical Power

Abundant and well-designed lighting can transform a plaza from a dim, foreboding space into a desirable, 24-hour amenity. Too often, however, light levels are excessively uneven or are dimmed in an effort to unofficially "close" a plaza. All public plazas are required to maintain two horizontal foot candles of illumination across all walkable and seating areas in the plaza and sidewalks adjacent to the public plaza. The minimum hours of illumination are from at least one hour before sunset to one hour after sunrise. This requirement applies to all plazas, regardless of whether the plaza has been permitted to close at night. All light sources mounted on or within buildings that illuminate the public plaza must be shielded from direct view. This prevents direct floodlighting of the plaza area, which can impair visibility and compromise the sense of safety. In addition, all lighting within the public plaza must be shielded to avoid effects on nearby residential units.

3.4 Litter Receptacles

Litter receptacles must be of sufficient size and quantity to accommodate typical plaza uses, such as lunchtime crowds in a Midtown plaza. One receptacle is required for every 1,500 square feet of plaza. Plazas greater than 6,000 square feet are required to provide an additional one receptacle for every additional 2,000 square feet of plaza. Plazas containing food service, such as open air cafés, are required to provide an additional receptacle for every 1,500 square feet of eating area. All receptacles must have a minimum capacity of 25 gallons and a minimum opening of 12 inches. To ensure that litter receptacles are located so as to adequately serve users of the plaza, all required seating areas must have a litter receptacle within 50 feet.

3.5 Bicycle Parking

In April 2009 the City Council adopted a Department of City Planning zoning text amendment that requires all new development to provide bicycle parking, including new buildings that utilize the public plaza bonus. However, bicycle parking can also serve plaza users that stop for lunch at an open air café, to shop at adjacent retail, or who simply need a rest. All public plazas must provide parking for at least two bicycles and plazas greater than 10,000 square feet in size must provide parking for at least four bicycles. To ensure that bicycle parking is readily accessible and well-used, bicycle parking is required to be located on the sidewalk adjacent to the public plaza. The New York City Department of Transportation has established standards for the placement of bicycle racks in the public sidewalk and evaluates all requests pursuant to this provision. The bicycle parking requirement may be waived if the Department of Transportation finds that its standards for placement of bicycle racks cannot be met.

3.6 Public Space Signage

The provision of clear, visible, and readable signage is essential to identify plazas as public spaces, to provide a list of required amenities provided within the plaza, and to identify hours of access and those responsible for the upkeep and maintenance of the plaza space.

(1) Design Regulations

The public plaza regulations include standard design guidelines for fonts, colors, and materials for all required public plaza signage. All required plaza signage must be constructed from highly durable materials such as metal or stone that are fully opaque and non-reflective. In addition, all text is required to be highly contrasting with the background color of the sign, at least three-quarters of an inch in height, and in a bold, non-narrow, and sans-serif font such as Verdana, Helvetica, or Arial.

The privately owned public space logo, a stylized tree on a gridded background, has been misrepresented and depicted incorrectly in existing plazas. The use of the digital POPS logo file in its original, unaltered form, is now required for all public space signage. The logo is required to be dark green or black in color and placed over a highly contrasting background color or material.

(2) Entry Plaque

The entry plaque is the primary plaza sign that identifies the space as public and part of the City's privately owned public space system. One entry plaque is required for every 40 linear feet of street frontage of the public plaza. The plaque is required to be located within five feet of the public sidewalk. The plaque must contain the text "Open to public", the International Symbol for Access, and "Open 24 hours" or the approved hours of access if a closing has been authorized.

(3) Informational Plaque

The informational plaque, provided either separately or as part of an entry plaque, is a critical tool in communicating the required amenities provided within the plaza, the entity responsible for plaza maintenance, and information on how to ask a question or file a complaint about a public plaza. Information plaques are required to be located within five feet of a public sidewalk and at least three feet above the level of the plaza. To identify the plaque as part of the plaza signage, the public space logo must be included. The information plaque is required to state the hours of operation of the plaza, the amount of required amenities, the name and contact information for the plaza owner, and direction to call 311 in the case of questions or complaints.

3.7 Additional Amenities

Plazas that exceed 5,000 square feet are required to provide amenities in addition to those described above. This requirement acknowledges that larger plazas can and should accommodate a more varied palette of design features. The additional amenities are: artwork; moveable tables and chairs; water features, such as fountains or reflecting pools; children's play areas; game tables and seating; and food service, such as open air cafés, kiosks, or food service in adjacent retail spaces. Plazas between 5,000 and 10,000 square feet are required to provide at least one of the additional amenities and plazas greater than 10,000 square feet must provide three. Plazas greater than 10,000 square feet in area and associated with a commercial building must provide food service as one of the three required additional amenities.

References
City of Chico, Principles of Good Plaza Design
New York City Department of City Planning, Current Public Plaza Standards

Dandenong Civic Centre

Location: Dandenong, Victoria, Australia
Area: 4,500m²
Completion Date: 2014
Landscape Design: rush\wright associates
Photography: Peter Bennetts , Chris Erskine, Michael Wright
Client: City of Greater Dandenong

The new Dandenong Municipal Building and Civic Centre is the new public heart of the rapidly changing and revitalized Central of Dandenong. The ensemble of community spaces, library, Council services and retail forms a public agora, a market place of community exchange and the primary address of the new city.

This ensemble holds at its centre a new civic square, a destination and new forum for the daily social commerce of the council, the new library, community meeting rooms and the uses proposed for the square itself. It is being designed for safe and enjoyable use at all hours, in all seasons.

The square also needs to accommodate larger scale events for groups and crowds of many sizes. For Dandenong's diverse community with a varied range of lifestyles and social values, the use of public space is very different. This is achieved by providing a main central 'open' space with maximum flexibility. Around this, about a dozen smaller spaces, each with their own character, are arranged. Then there is events programming, and appropriate levels of commercial activation to provide the requisite dignified balance between the civic and the commercial.

The design explores the idea of the cosmopolitan city center, a place for all people to share a unique experience of belonging in Australia. Forms, patterns, and shapes are being explored that may echo an archaeology of cultural experience, from the living culture of the traditional Wurundjeri owners through to the life experience of those from Africa, Asia, the Middle East, and

Aerial photo of Civic Center urban context

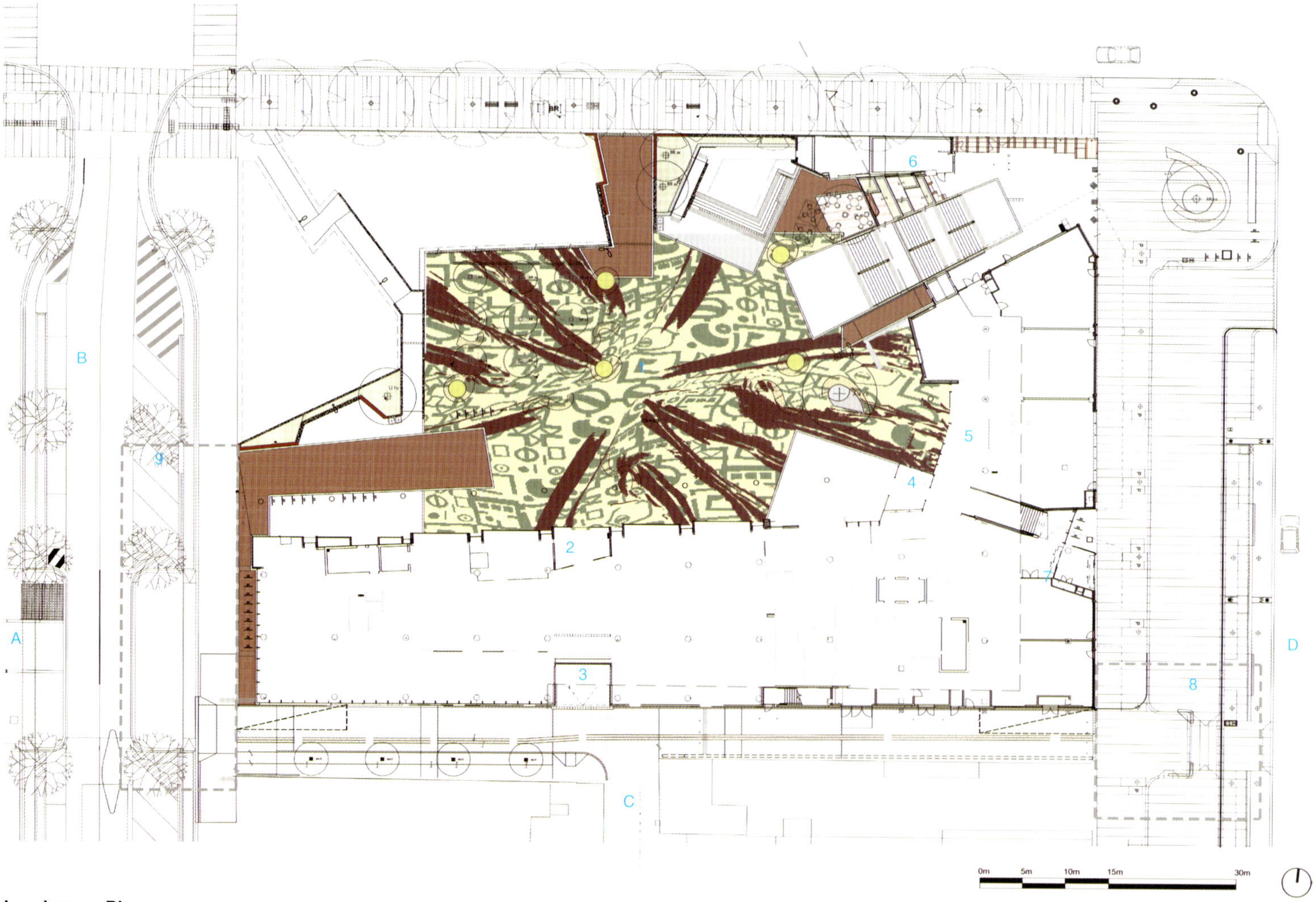

Landscape Plan

1. Civic square
2. Library entry from civic square
3. Car park entry from lane
4. Library entry from civic aquare
5. Library entry from civic aquare
6. Retail
7. Council oddices / entry street level
8. Integration works: zone E
9. Integration works: zone B

A. City Street
B. Thomas Street
C. Kingsbury Lane
D. Lonsdale Street

View Looking West South West
1. New municipal building
2. Lonsdale Street
3. New library building
4. Loggia
5. The grove
6. Main square
7. Main stairs
8. Micro plaza
9. Walker Street
10. Stage and screen retail below
11. Tem porary grass
12. Thomas Street

elsewhere. The design explores the potential of surfaces, walls, steps, seats, and plantings to suggest a series of 'found objects' that may be evocative of the history of the site, the settlement of Dandenong, the recent alterations in built form, and the richness of the exotic.

This project creates an opportunity to establish a unique arboreal landscape for Central Dandenong. As the centerpiece of the municipality, there is space for large trees. The ambition is to plant trees which are unusual, grand, and which will play a prominent civic role, creating long lasting markers and memorable living monuments that contribute actively to the sense of civic pride and expression on the site.

The Main Square

1. Micro plaza
2. Main stairs
3. Loggia
4. Main square
5. Stage and screen
6. Walker street service entry
7. The grove
8. Temporary grass

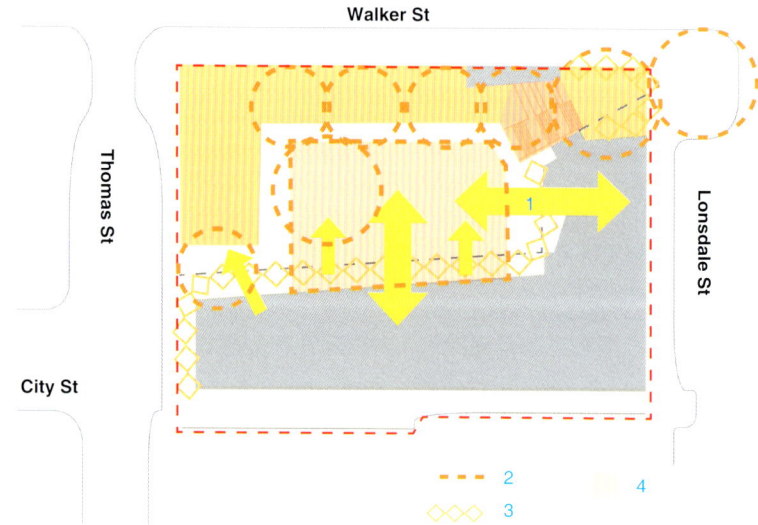

Outdoor Rooms

1. Council chamber room
2. Outdoor rooms
3. Material integrations
4. Main square

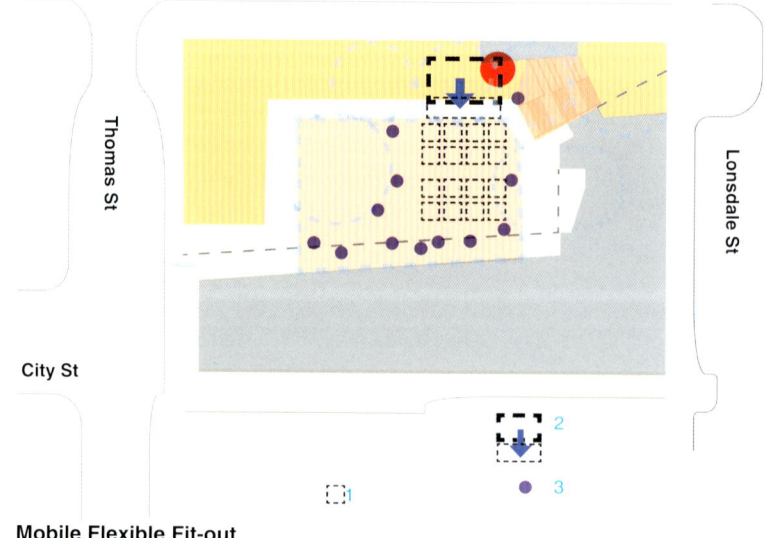

Mobile Flexible Fit-out

1. 4m x 4m umbrellas which can be moved at will
2. Civic stage extension area
3. Large scale furntiture items which can be moved around with a forklift from time to time

Stage and Screen

1. Walker Street
2. Entry into plaza
3. Stage and screen
4. Main square
5. Main stairs
6. Temporary umbrellas

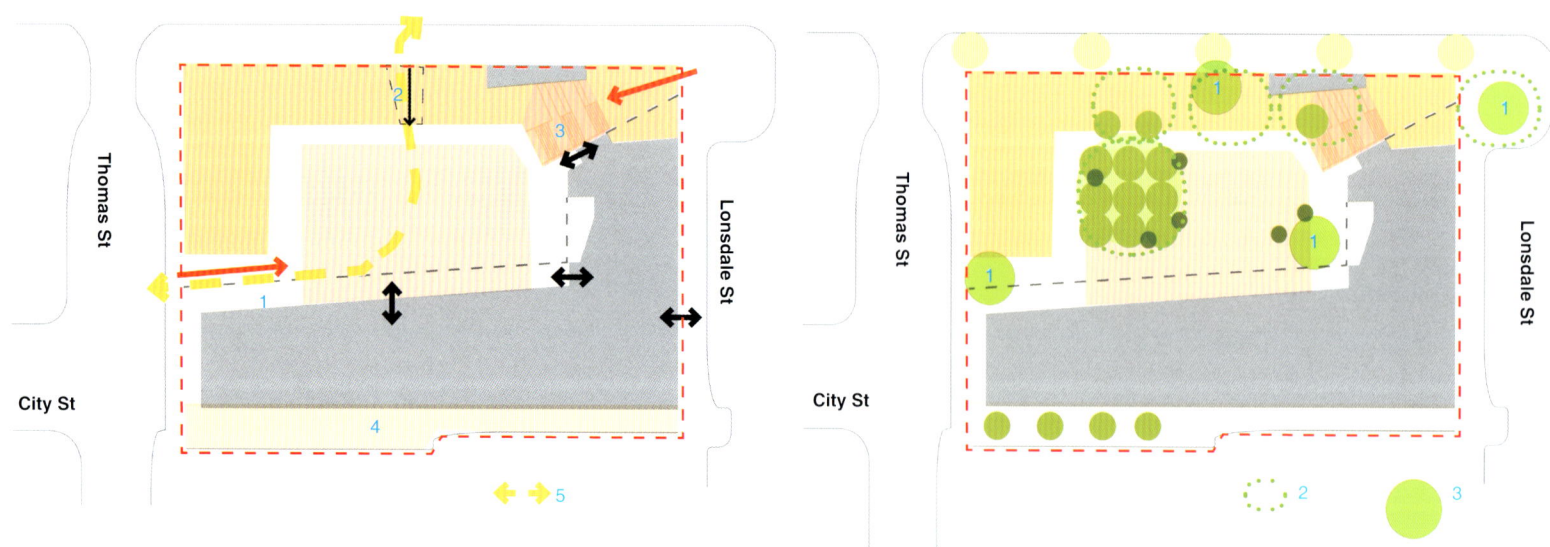

New across temporary grass area.

Permeability and Access Walker Street

1. At grade
2. 1:80 entry
3. Steps SML+LRG
4. 1:S27 Grad fall to Lonsdale Street
5. Emergency / service while access

Trees and Planting

1. Entry
2. Integrated planting permeable surfaces
3. Trees

View towards historic town hall

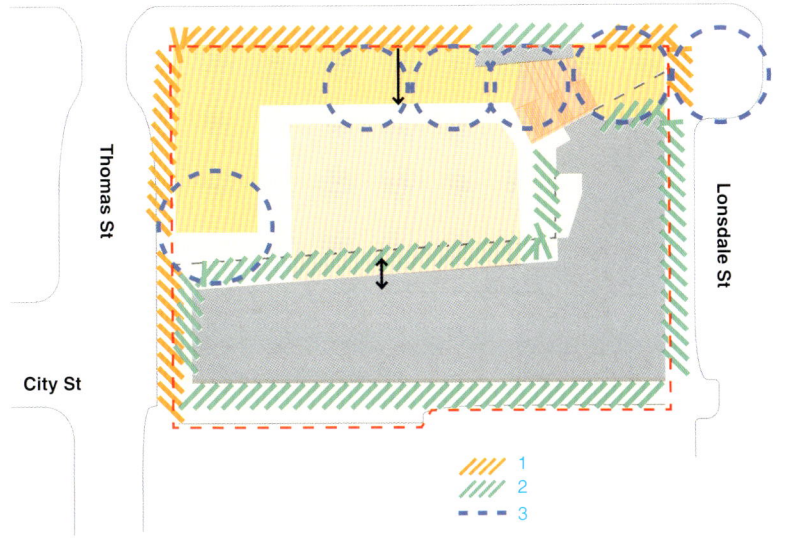

Urban Activity

1. Street front
2. Building edge
3. Edge zone space

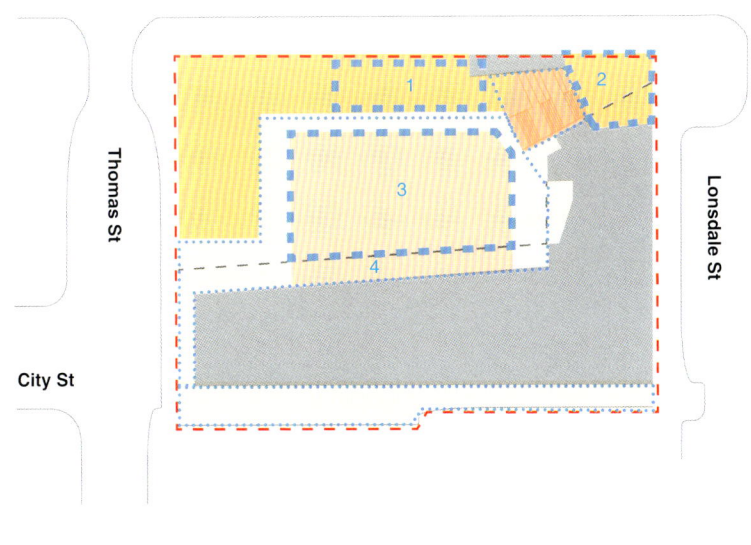

Scale of Spaces

1. 2400m² Edge zone = 500m² "outdoor rooms"
2. 224m²
3. St. central zone = 1250m² with outer circulation = 2400m² edge
4. 224m² circulation zone walker

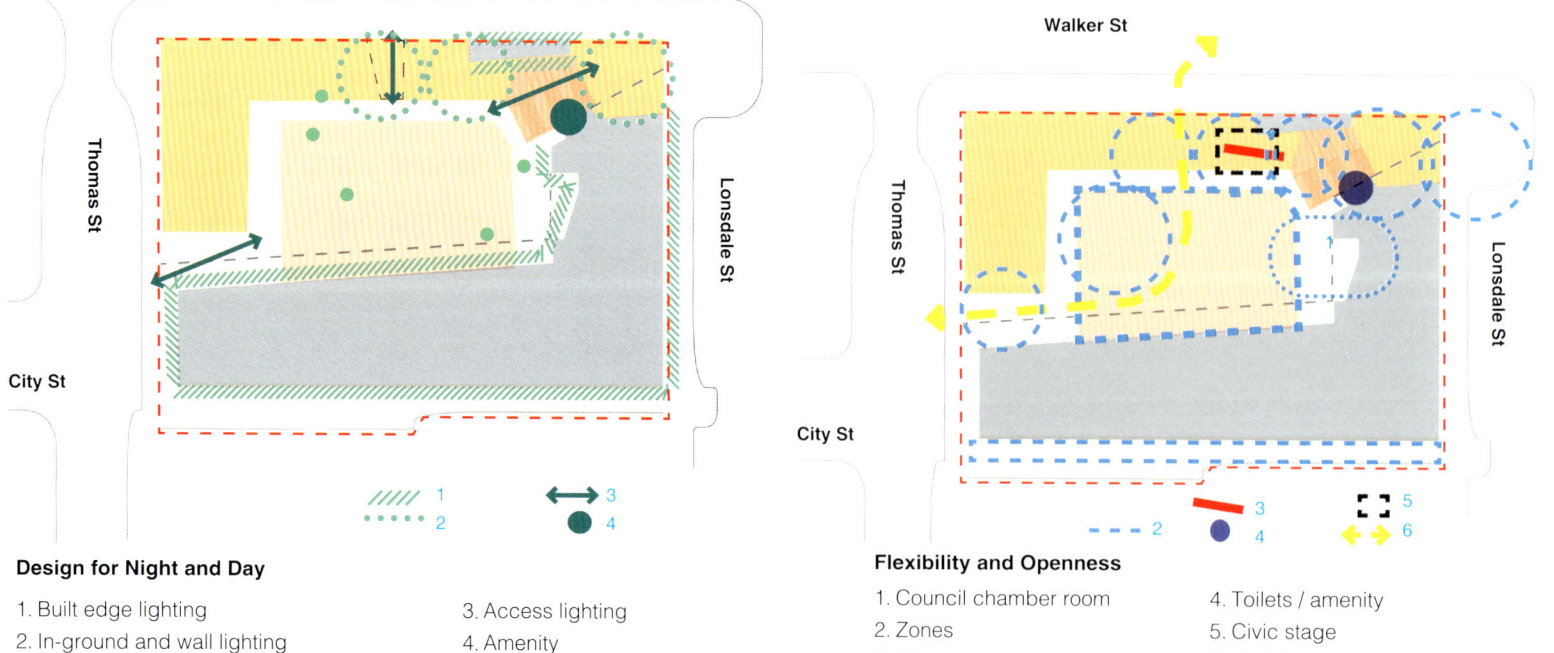

New across temporary grass area

Design for Night and Day

1. Built edge lighting
2. In-ground and wall lighting
3. Access lighting
4. Amenity

Flexibility and Openness

1. Council chamber room
2. Zones
3. Big screen
4. Toilets / amenity
5. Civic stage
6. Vehicle access

113

Reconstruction of the Square in Frýdlant

Location: Frýdlant, Czech Republic
Area: 4,000m²
Completion Date: 2011
Landscape Design: Vladimír Balda
Photography: Aleš Jungmann, Jiří Jiroutek
Client: Frýdlant City Government

The main idea behind the design of the reconstructed square in Frýdlant was to create an open, unobstructed public space – a square that allows residents and visitors to enjoy all types of activities. The use of three types of paving tiles, two types of stone and the patterns in which these were laid differentiates various types of spaces on the square. With the exception of the parking lot, the square was realized as a barrier-free space.

This dominant feature of the square is situated along its north side on an axis with Kostelní Street and divides the central part of the square into two halves. The divided square can be used for various purposes such as fairs, concerts, and theatrical performances. The central part of the square is clearly defined by a distinct type of dark basalt tiles, new public lighting and town installations such as information panels, benches, waste bins, bike stands, and a drinking fountain, which are placed around its perimeter. The uniform basalt surface also features the outline of the former town hall made from the original basalt cobblestones. The foundations of the Renaissance town hall were discovered by an archaeological excavation during the reconstruction of the square.

The space in front of the current town hall in the northwest part of the square is a representative area for the gathering of citizens. A mobile stage can be installed in the open space next to four wooden flag pole stands featuring the town crest.

Site Plan

Located on the opposite, southeast side of the square with sycamore trees and benches are cafés and restaurants with outdoor summer seating. The two opposite ends of the square are both paved with the same large granite paving tiles.

The historical parcelization of the square is reflected in an abstract manner in the small granite tiles of the pavements around the central part of the square. Paths for car traffic and parking spaces on the northeast and southwest sides of the square are differentiated from pedestrian paths by a distinct granite tile pattern.

Top: Front view of the square.
Bottom: Detail of the flagpoles.

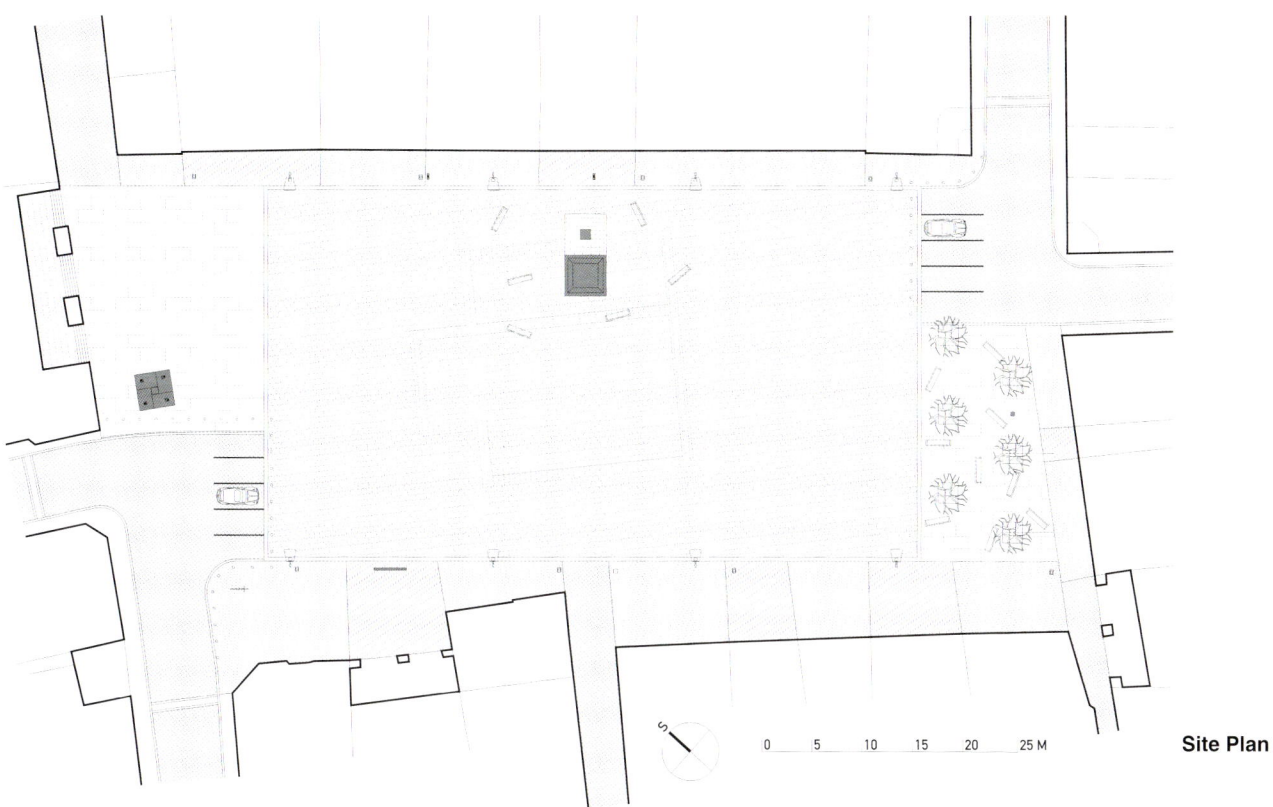

Site Plan

Hoekenrode Square

Location: Amsterdam, the Netherlands
Area: 170,000m²
Completion Date: 2013 - 2014
Landscape Design: karres en brands landschap architecture+urban planning
Photography: karres en brands landschap architecture+urban planning
Client: Municipality of Amsterdam

Hoekenrode Square is the connecting link between shopping area Amsterdamse Poort and leisure area Arena Boule-vard. With the redevelopment of the Nieuw Amsterdam building, the square is one of the last phases of the ArenaPoort Centre district to be developed. The building has been extended and a hotel, cafés and other public functions are situated in the plinth. With its favorable location close to the Bijlmer Arena station, the Arena A soccer stadium, several hotels, bars, shops, and restaurants, Hoekenrode Square might be the most important city square of Amsterdam Zuid-Oost.

The design is based on logical pedestrian connection through the area and existing level differences. Granite edges solve the level differences, guide pedestrians, and make spaces for terraces on the square. The floor of ceramic bricks in different color mixes and the granite edges connect to the designs of Arena Boulevard and Amsterdamse Poort shopping area. On reserved area for a future pavilion on the square, a grass hill is now situated, offering long views through the area, a suitable spots for performance stages or a place to lie in the grass. In the main pedestrian connection a special light and water feature is situated. During daytime its lifted edges and water features invite people to sit and play; at night it transforms into an interactive light feature.

A special part of the overall design is the Smart Light lighting design which during night time offers different atmospheres on the square. In collaboration with Lichtvormgevers, Philips and Cisco Karres en Brands made the design for the dynamic and interactive lighting of the square. For each sort of use of the square a different light scenario with specific atmospheres has

Section

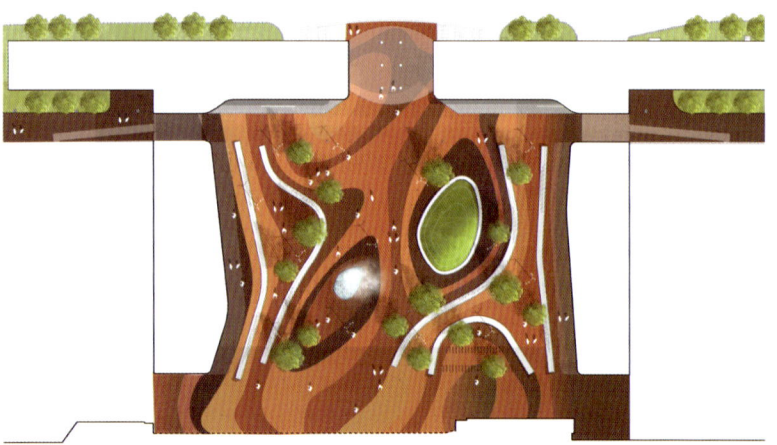
Plan

Natural stone elements provide pleasant seating.

been composed. The character of the square thus varies from a night life leisure area to a functional passage space for commuters or a catchment area for soccer fans. By means of crowd sensors the lighting schemes adjust to the current type of use of the square.

Hoekenrode Square Situated between the Arena Boulevard and the Amsterdamse Poort

1. Arena Boulevard
2. Poort Hoekenrode Square
3. Amsterdamse Poort

Top: The road pavement in gray and brown
Opposite: The stone stairs for seats in the square

Leyteire Courtyard

Location: Université Victor Segalen-Bordeaux, French
Area: 2,700 m²
Completion Date: 2012
Landscape Design: Anouk Debarre Landscape Architect
Architecture Design: Martin Duplantier Architect
Lighting Design: Anton Y. Olano
Photography: Arthur Péquin and Yohan Zerdoun
Client: University of Bordeaux

The Operation Campus, a nation wide university redevelopment plan, begins with urban design at its heart: scenery of fluxes, terraces of an anthropology museum, and a negative space of an amphitheater with too narrow corridors. This square hosts new and numerous functions, mostly informal, that make out the life of a "real" campus.

A place of urbanity and fertility, a landmark for a new vision for university campuses.

The project develops three different formal elements:

1. Green world: Inserting vegetation is done through all its forms: on green walls, on flush areas, on a grid, deep in the ground.

2. Canopy: a new canopy will develop itself between the buildings, creating new views, new light filters and shadows. As a consequence, the heat effect is reduced, and the temperature comfort zone is improved.

3. From intimate to public show. The project is organized through a central open space with a public scene, leaving more intimate peripheral spaces on the sides. This spatial hierarchy creates a diverse thus coherent entity, able to host different functions for an urban university: shows and celebrations, group work, all sunny recreational spaces.

The plan is segmented through a series of identical rectangles: topography is the main thread of a rain drop flowing towards an

The front view of the courtyard.

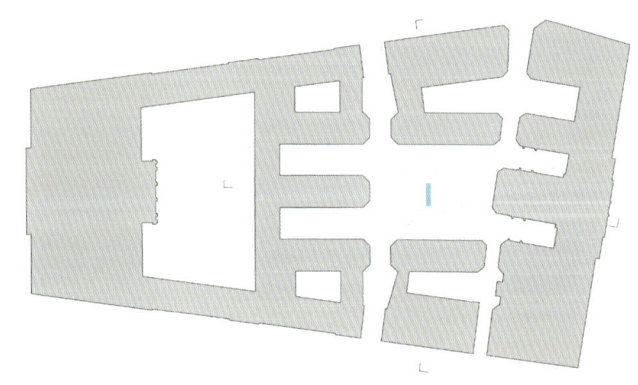

Ground Plan

upraised basin. This basin reflects the surrounding architecture of the 19th century, the planted trees, the breath of wind.

The 80cm wide strips integrate simple concrete furniture and planted areas, providing a welcoming shade on these central spaces.

A chromatic strategy has allowed a soft and elegant atmosphere to invade this former delivery square to become the central spot for informal meetings in the heart of this historical university.

The heart of the university is alive again.

The stone stairs in black and gray in the courtyard.

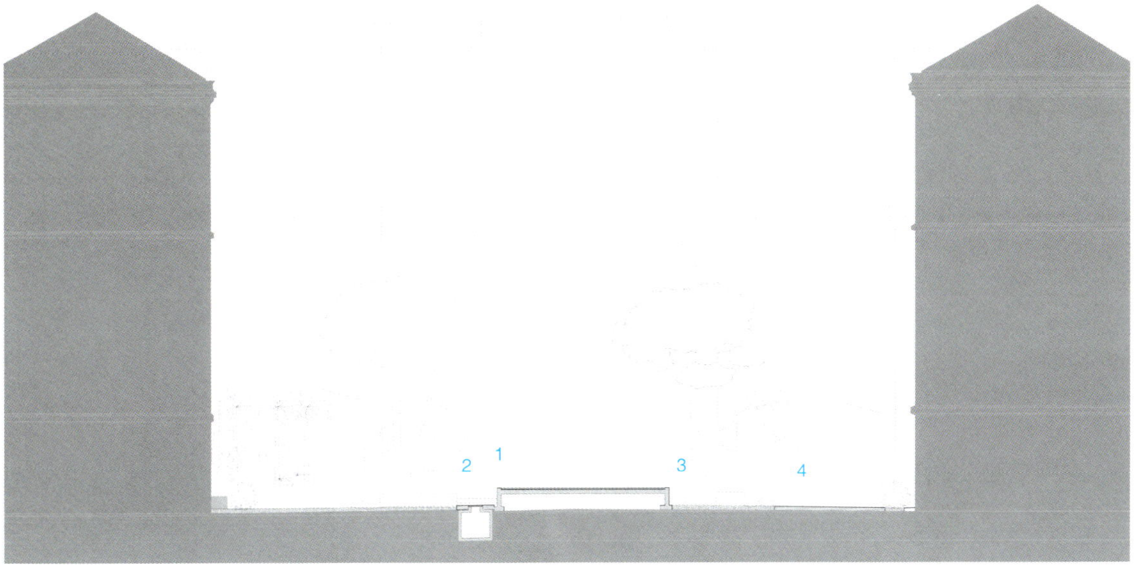

Detail Section and Legends

1. Water table of tinted polished concrete
2. Water gutter channel
3. Broomed and colored concrete floor
4. Deactivated and coloured concrete floor

Transversal Section A

Longitudinal Section B

Mechelen Centrumimpuls

Location: London, United Kingdom
Area: 1,500m²
Completion Date: 2014
Landscape Architect: OKRA
Photography: OKRA
Client: Gemeente Mechelen

The public space within the city of Mechelen has been greatly renovated in recent years, undergoing a real metamorphosis: from anonymous city to a destination. Mechelen Centrum impuls has had an important role in this transformation. For each of the projects within the Centre impuls an integrated approach towards archaeology, mobility on land and on water, tourism and regeneration of the city center are all represented in our approach, vision and realized in the specific designs. The centrumimpuls consists of a number of individual projects comprising the Melaan, Sint Katelijnestraat, Hoogstraat-Korenmarkt, Lange Schipstraat, and the Vlietenkelder. All designed by OKRA Landscape Architects.

In 2005 within the framework of the European Initiative Water in Historic city centers, OKRA started by opening up the Melaan in Mechelen. After Melaan the Sint Katelijnestraat was redesigned by OKRA where the stream is represented at the Stadsheimelijkheid (square) by a large water table. On the floor is a beautiful accent line with the typical droplet pattern, which can also be found on the seat edge of the Melaan. These accent lines mark the streams that cannot be opened. Besides the Melaan and the water table in the Sint Katelijnestraat, OKRA designs the stream in the Zelestraat where part of the stream again will be opened in the street. In addition, a shorter length of the vault of the stream is made visible as part of showing the historical stratification of Mechelen.

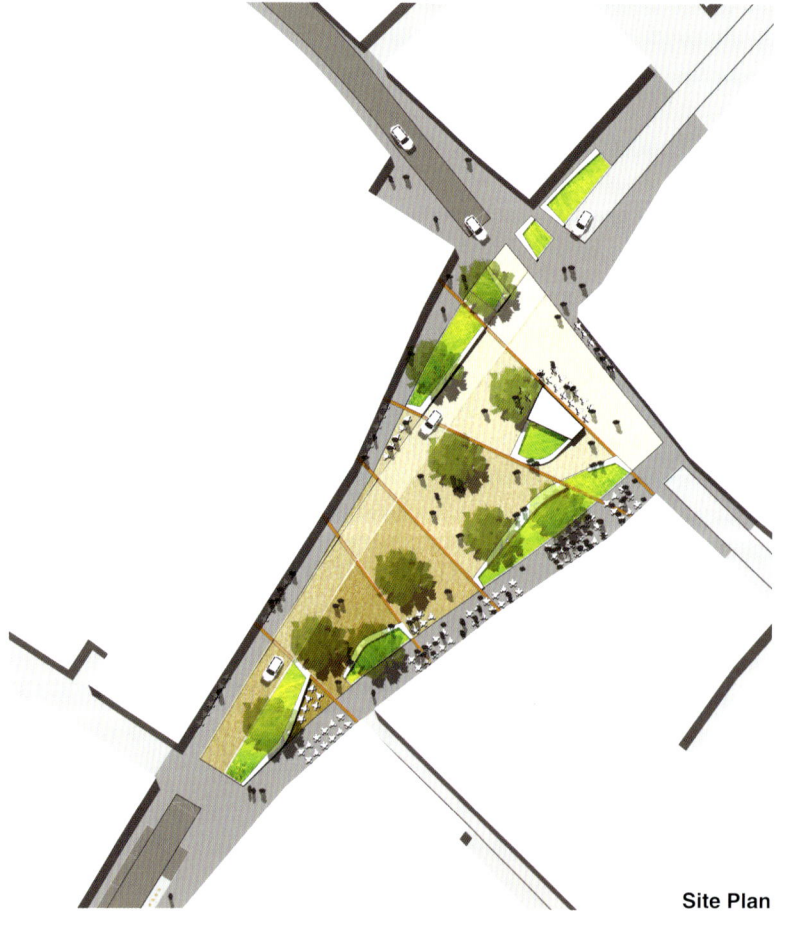

Site Plan

The flower bed in front of the buildings.

Underneath the IJzerenleen is also a former stream. By transforming the vault underneath the IJzerenleen into Vliet Cellar a piece of history and an old stream is again revealed in the city center. In the vault of the stream is a large room, which serves as an exhibition space.

Mechelen Centrum impuls encompasses more than just making visible the invisible and thus reducing the flow in the streets of the city. It is also about defining space types and making qualitative public space. In the urban fabric urban radians play an important role. Sint Katelijnestraat with the other adjacent square around the Sint Katelijne Church and the Hoogstraat starting at the Brusselse Poort to the Dijle are radials already redone. And the Lange Schipstraat, the southern shore, has been redesigned with special attention to the relationship with the Dijle.

In addition to the projects that mainly revolve around creating length and tangible curved the pattern of the urban fabric, a number of qualitative spaces at the center of Mechelen were

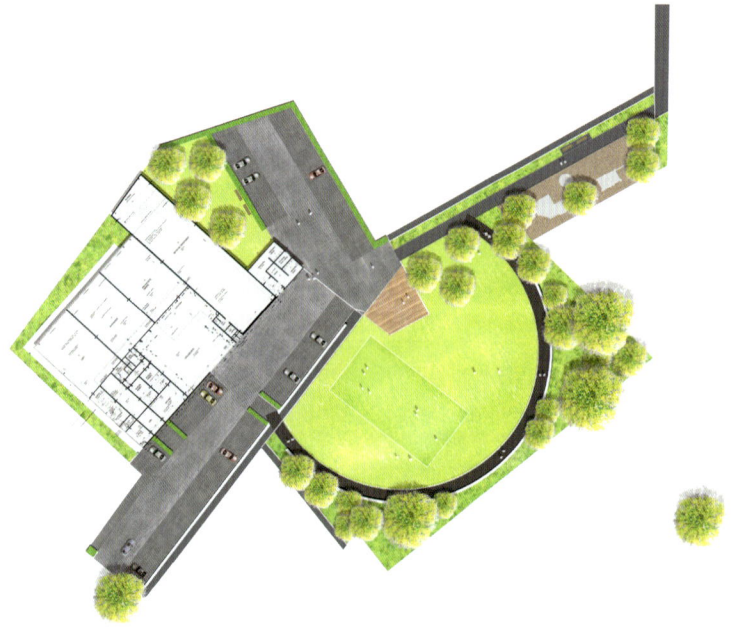

Site Plan

The street square for the residents.

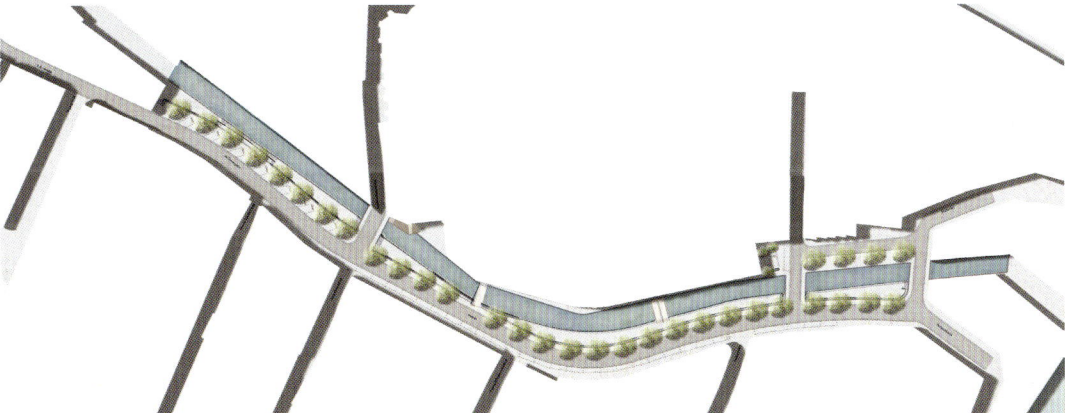

The Plan of the Street

added. We can mention the small stack along the Lange Schipstraat, Sint Katelijne Cemetery, de Stadsheimelijkheid, the Ganzendries as well as also the Korenmarkt. The Korenmarkt is a square with many great historical meaning. It is one of the oldest squares of the city from which the city was created, the dry sand ridge and was in earlier days an important trading place for amongst others grain. OKRA designed the square so that the height difference to the Dijle tangible is made visible because it is a stepped square. The sand colored floor refers to the sand surface and the grain that was traded here. The Korenmarkt is again a destination. A place to enjoy and, above all, a square for the residents.

Above: The main road
Opposite: The rest spaces in the square in sunshine

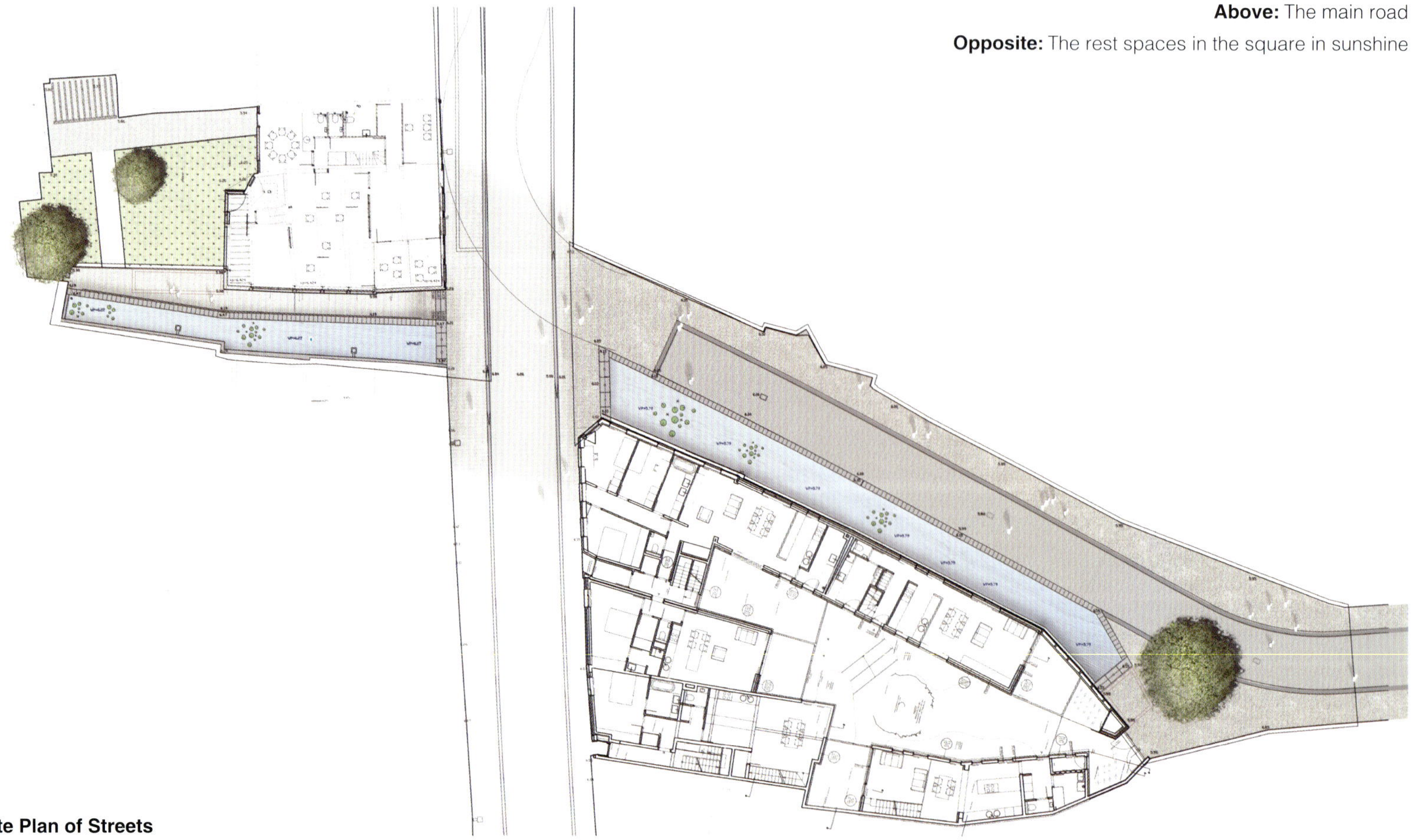

Site Plan of Streets

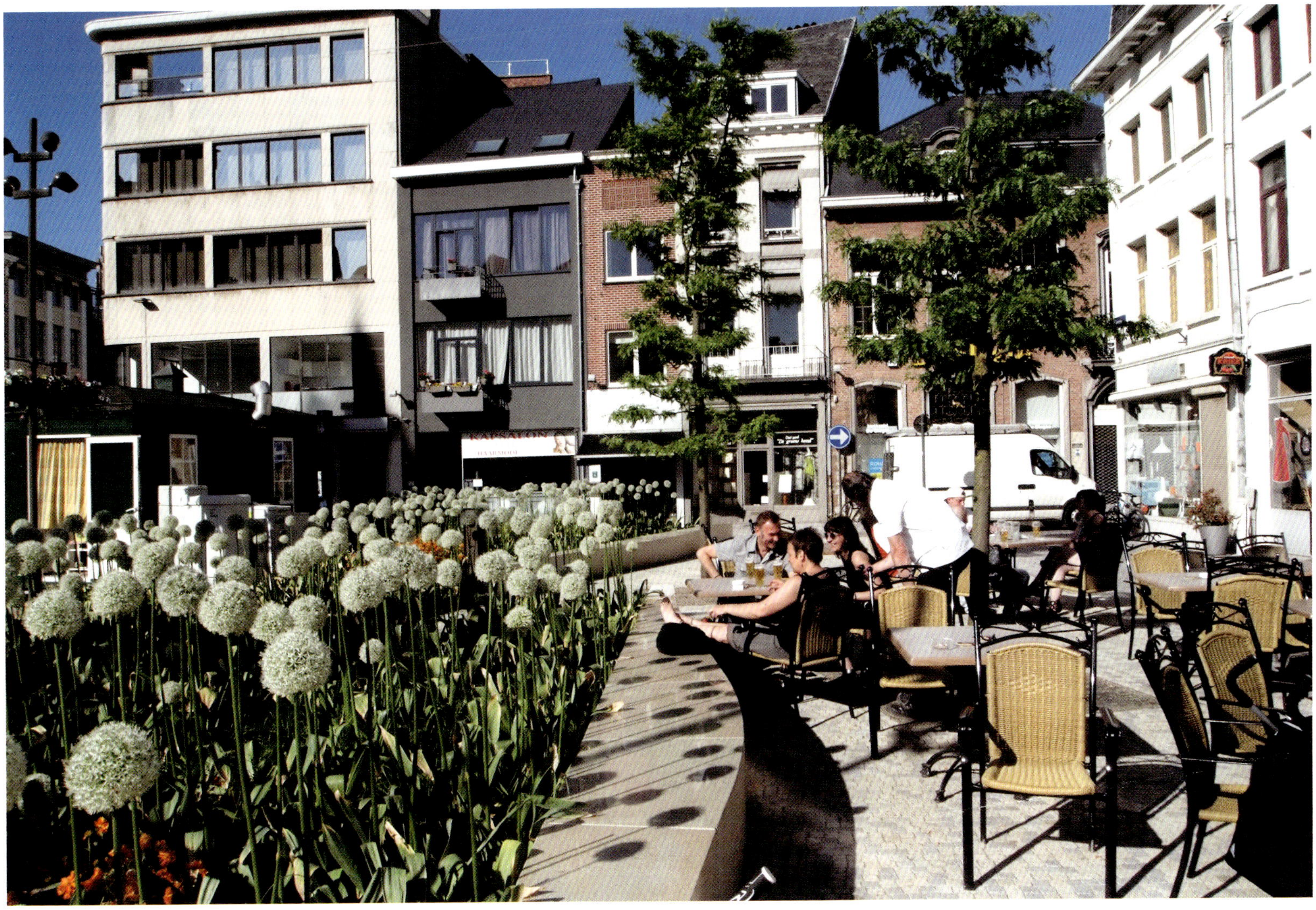

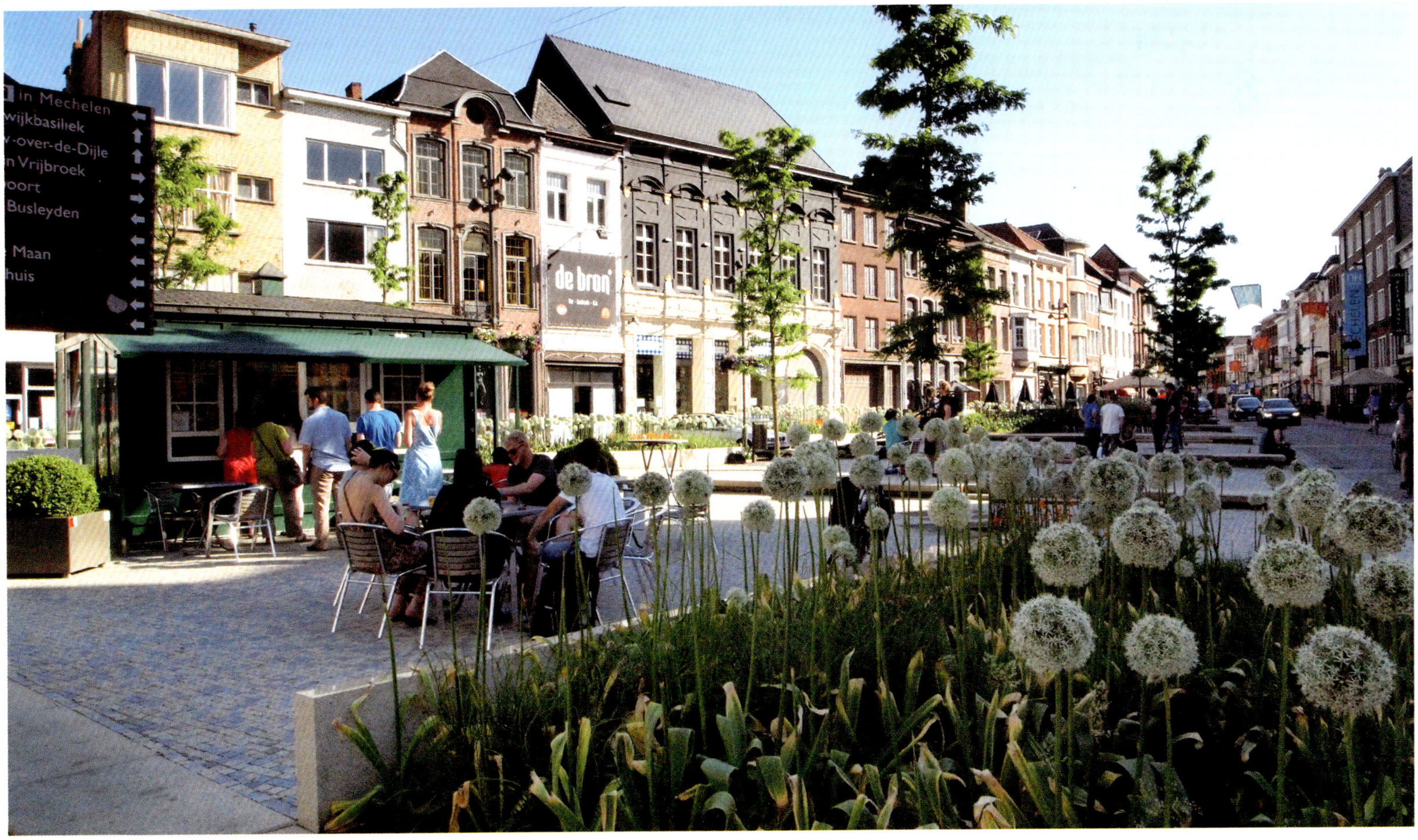
in Mechelen
wijkbasiliek
-over-de-Dijle
Vrijbroek
Busleyden
Maan
huis
de bron

Above: The tree grids and flower beds along the river.
Opposite: The entrance of the underground tunnel.

Place d'Austerlitz in Strasbourg

Location: Strasbourg, French
Area: 9,900m²
Completion Date: 2012
Photographer: DIGITALEpaysage
Client: Ville de Strasbourg et Communauté Urbaine de Strasbourg
Design Company: Amiot-Lombard architectes / landscape designer DIGITALEpaysage / Samuel Lollier Ingénierie / Lighting Consultant Coup d'Eclat

Place d'Austerlitz, the former Porte des Bouchers, is a much frequented hub between the old city and the "Heyritz Kehl" urban thorough fare in the making.

The aim of this project consists of making the place a veritable living space to be appropriated by the inhabitants of four districts, of which it is the hub, without denying its transit function: operating on a city scale, but also on a neighbourhood and individual level, and making passage and motion the conceptual material of the project.

Movement is imprinted in the composition; like a text, it engraves the pattern of our movements on the base that receives sit. We are making two types of space and two types of use coexist: the urban basis of movement and cross flow, and the freer and less constricted garden which provides temporary relief from the city; the garden as refuge, a garden for leisure.

There is a harmonious encounter between the geometry of the mineral-of architecture, and theorganic forms of the living, assymbolised by the circle-gardens.

An archipeli ago of nature between the historic and the modern city.

The gardens are "extramural" implantantations, beyond the symbolic limit drawn by the new gate – evoking the ancient wall

Site Plan

of Strasbourg. The living aspect is expressed through the circle, in contrast to the urban minerality of the place. Each circle hosts more than the resistance of nature in an urban milieu. Each circle weaves friendship, we are talking about the place of the living in the city, the relationship between it and man, and their harmonious coexistence at the dawn of the third millennium.

1. Green joint
2. Foundation in 30cm polymer concrete
3. Gutter

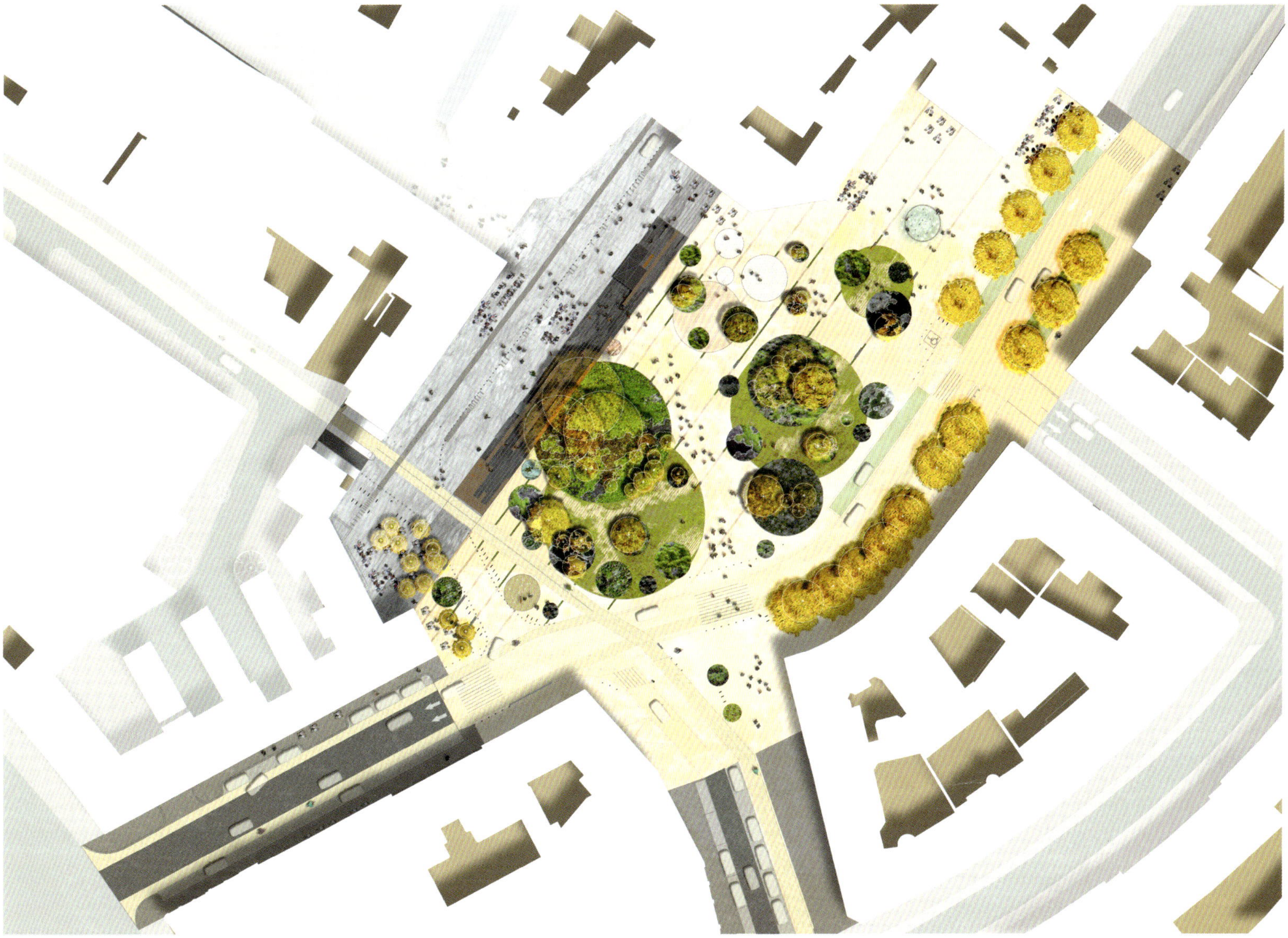

The furniture drawn by the architects Amiot-Lombard.

Bruno Steiner's Sketch

Above: May, 2014
Bottom left: Main axis
Bottom right: Preserved existing trees

Golden Gate Bridge 75th Anniversary Plaza

Location: California, United States
Area: 4,452m²
Completion Date: 2012
Landscape Design: SURFACEDESIGN INC
Photography: Marion Brenner, James A.Lord
Client: Golden Gate National Parks Conservancy
Awards: Cultural Landscape Foundation Award Golden gate Plaza and Lands' End lookout 2012;
Engineering News Record award winner for the Golden Gate Bridge Plaza;
The Cultural Landscape Foundation, Golden Gate National Parks: What's Out There, March 2013.

The Golden Gate Bridge, a San Francisco icon, spans the foggy bay, connecting the city and the majestic Marin Headlands. A new plaza created for the 75th Anniversary of the bridge enhances access and visibility of the breathtaking Golden Gate and San Francisco Bay. This new public space and accompanying Visitor Center honor the bridge as they tell the story of its creation, emerging as a new cultural and ecological hub at the bay's edge.

The project creates a prominent pavilion for exhibiting historic artifacts previously not accessible to the public. The Plaza and Visitor Center provides space for expanded exhibits showcasing the design and engineering of the bridge. Among these exhibits is a new and prominent location for a statue of bridge engineer Joseph Strauss, emphasizing his important role in the conception of the bridge. Formerly a parking lot obscured by vegetation, the new Cable Overlook features a cross section of the bridge cable oriented inline with the bridge and never before seen views of the bay and bridge.

The layout and design of the plaza itself is a study in the marvel of the bridge's engineering. The narrow proportions of the central plaza echo the slender scale and dimensions of the bridge

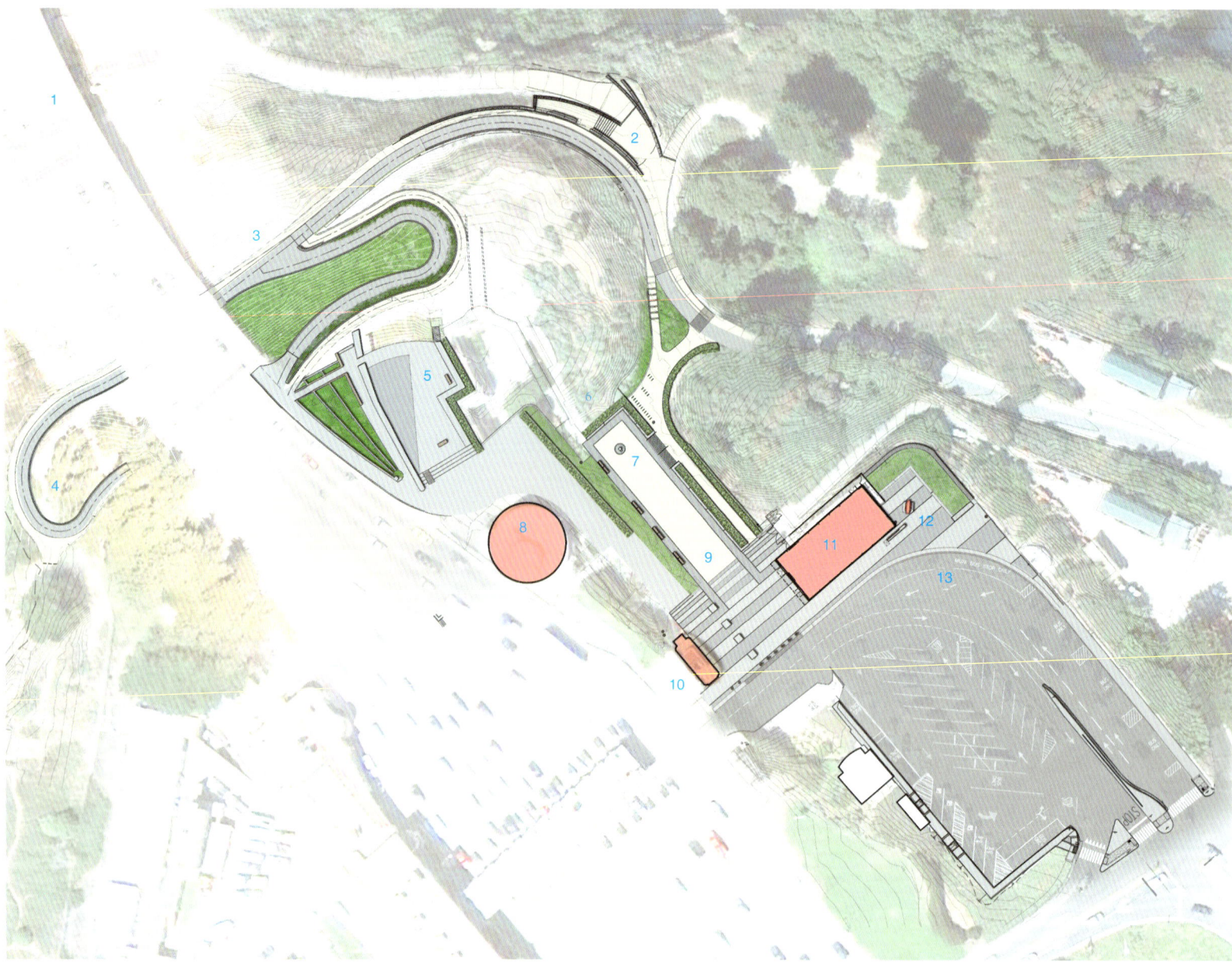

Golden Gate Bridge Plaza Plan

1. Golden Gate Bridge
2. Fort Point overlook
3. Battery east bay trail
4. Bay trail west loop
5. Flag pole plaza
6. Battery Lancaster
7. Strauss sculpture
8. Roundhouse
9. Golden Gate Bridge Plaza
10. Café
11. Visitors pavilion
12. Cable overlook
13. Bus dropoff

towers. Visitors will notice an alternating pattern of light and dark pavers that mirror the shadows of the cables as they recede into the distance across the bridge. The long transverse bands made up of narrow module pavers are reminiscent of the massive cables supporting the bridge, which are themselves composed of many narrow gauge cables.

The bridge is undeniably beautiful as an icon, but it is only when animated by visitors and commuters that it is truly majestic and a part of the cultural landscape. The project presents a new outdoor living room for the city along with the first on-site center dedicated to telling the stories of the bridge and its creation. The design also provides coordinated and safe modes for people to arrive and unload from buses and cars and presents a new access route for cyclists for easier movement. The new design reconfigures the site and existing topography to provide ADA access to the plaza as well as the bridge. Pedestrian and bicycle traffic are separated for safety and the new paths provide a remarkable launch for strolling across the bridge or for a bike ride to Marin. In addition, newly graded trails promote safe bicycle commuting, connecting to the Bay Trail network around the bay.

Top: Once relegated to a corner and hard to reach, this section of cable now has a place of honor, overlooking the bridge.

Bottom: Formerly a parking lot obscured by vegetation, a formal space featuring the cable provides a place for gatherings and celebrations with never before seen views of the San Francisco Bay and the Golden Gate Bridge.

Top: Concrete seat benches serve a dual function. Designed to delineate safe zones for pedestrians and bikes, the benches also act as platforms for performances and photographs.

Bottom: The previously inaccessible northern edge of the city provides amazing views of Fort Point, the Bay, and the Golden Gate Bridge. The paths create a romantic place to stroll and watch the ships arrive and depart beneath the iconic bridge.

Opposite top: The pavilion was built simultaneously with the plaza and it represents a new visitor center typology for the National Park Service, incorporating interpretative retail outlets that engage with the site's history.

Opposite bottom: The new design highlights Battery Lancaster and creates a space for the statue of Joseph Strauss, the bridge's engineer. The benches incorporate the steel vocabulary from the bridge and the wood is repurposed from military-planted trees in the Presidio.

Chapter 3 Waterfront Public Open Space Design

The Guiding Principles of the Waterfront Edge Design Guidelines define a set of core values for best design practices for the waterfront edge. A well-designed edge is one where waterfront access, resilience, and ecological benefits are all incorporated into an integrated design. As a tool to guide and enhance new projects on an elective basis, waterfront edge design guidelines should feature design concepts that are buildable, understandable, cost effective, and can meet regulations. While each site and project has its own characteristics and goals guiding its outcome, the principles set forth provide a framework for which the guidelines will be created utilizing input from a multi disciplinary team and end-users.

1. Basic Principles and Functions for Waterfront Design

1.1 Create a Waterfront for All

The Central Waterfront should engage the entire city. It is a public asset and should remain focused on public use and activities that attract people from all walks of life. It should be a place for locals and visitors alike – a place where everything comes together and co-mingles effortlessly. The process for developing a waterfront design should, in fact must, draw on the talents and dreams of the entire city. The resulting public spaces and surrounding development will engage us through a range of activities throughout the day and year.

1.2 Put the Shoreline and Innovative, Sustainable Design at the Forefront

To succeed, the waterfront must bring people to the water's edge allowing them to experience the water itself and the unique geography and ecology. At the same time, we must take bold steps to improve the natural shoreline ecology while also preserving and enhancing the maritime activities that remain central to the Central Waterfront. The waterfront should, in its design, construction, and operation, reflect city's commitment to sustainability, innovation and responding to climate change.

(1) Enhance Ecology

Waterfront edge designs should protect existing aquatic habitat values and enhance designs, materials, and shore line arrangements to improve the ecological function of the coastal zone and strive to be consistent with regional ecological goals .

(2) Use A Science-Based, Evaluative Process for Restoration

Project decision makers should use all available science regarding ecological features of waterfront edge design. Projects with innovative ecological features should be monitored based on evidence in the literature and pre-project and/or baseline ecological site conditions to determine their effectiveness. Monitoring data should be used to improve designs over time.

(3) Promote Resiliency

Waterfront edge designs must accommodate, mitigate, or be adaptable to the effects of sea level rise and increased coastal flooding. Increases in precipitation may lead to increased stormwater runoff, and green infrastructure and planted edge design can play an important role in improving water quality.

(4) Enhance Public Access, Especially for Boats

Waterfront edge design should incorporate good public access designs which accommodate the highest number of uses including the widest range of boat types that closely reflect user input. Ensure waterfront edge designs do not preclude adding features that improve public access in the future. Recreation and opportunities to support human interaction with the water should be encouraged where appropriate.

2. Design Requirements for Waterfront Public Access Areas

2.1 General Provisions Applying to Waterfront Public Access Areas

(1) General Requirments

All waterfront public access areas shall be unobstructed from their lowest level to the sky. The lowest level of any portion of a waterfront public access area shall be determined by the elevation of the adjoining portion on the same or an adjoining zoning lot or the public sidewalk to which it connects. Reference elevations shall be established from the public sidewalks, waterfront yard levels and the elevations previously established by adjoining zoning lots at lot line intersections of a waterfront public access network, as applicable. The minimum required circulation path shall be connected and continuous through all waterfront public access areas on adjacent zoning lots. Waterfront public access areas shall be accessible to persons with physical disabilities in accordance with the Americans with Disabilities Act and the American National Standards Institute (ANSI) design guidelines.

(2) All Waterfront Public Access Areas Improved for Public Shall Meet the Following Regulations for Site Grading

In required circulation paths: for cross-sectional grading regulations (perpendicular to the general direction of pedestrian movement), the minimum slope of a required circulation path shall be one and one-half percent to allow for positive drainage and the maximum slope shall be three percent. Steps and stairways accommodating a cross-sectional grade change are only permitted outside of the required circulation path(s). For longitudinal grading controls (parallel to the general direction of pedestrian movement), grade changes shall be permitted along the length of a required circulation path by means of steps or ramps in compliance with the requirements for handicapped accessibility.

In required planting areas, including screening buffers: within 5 feet of the edge of any planting area, the grade level of such planting area shall be no more than 18 inches higher or lower than the adjoining level of the pedestrian circulation path.

(3) Vehicle and Emergency Access

Vehicular access is prohibited within waterfront public access areas except for emergency and maintenance vehicular access. Parking areas, passenger drop-offs, driveways, loading berths and building trash storage facilities are not permitted within, or allowed to be accessed or serviced through, a waterfront public access area, except for vehicular access to drop-offs and other required services accessory to docking facilities or to development on a pier or floating structure.

Such vehicular ways shall be used only to provide access across the shore public walkway. No single driveway shall exceed a width of 25 feet. A minimum 12 inch paved border shall be installed along the driveway boundaries and shall have a color distinct from the paving of the adjoining paved surface.

2.2 Design Requirements for Shore Public Walkways and Supplemental Public Access Areas

The design requirements of this Section shall apply to shore public walkways and supplemental public access areas.

(1) Circulation and Access

In all districts, a shore public walkway shall provide a circulation path with a minimum clear width of 12 feet. Such path shall be located within 10 feet of the shoreline for at least 20 percent of the length of such shoreline, and the remainder of the path may be located anywhere within the shore public walkway or supplemental public access area. Secondary paths, when provided, shall be at least 6 feet wide. When two circulation paths are parallel to each other, they shall be connected by other paths or accessible lawn at intervals not to exceed 200 feet. In order to facilitate the future connection of pedestrian circulation paths, where a shore public walkway is on a zoning lot that is adjacent to a zoning lot without a shore public walkway, the portion of the circulation path that terminates at the common zoning lot line shall be located within 30 feet of the shoreline.

A supplemental public access area shall provide at least one circulation path with a minimum clear width of 6 feet that provides access throughout the supplemental public access area. This requirement may be met by a circulation path of the shore public walkway that traverses the supplemental public access area.

(2) Seating

One linear foot of seating shall be provided for every 75 square feet of shore public walkway and supplemental public access area. Such seating may be located anywhere within such public access areas. In addition, up to 25 percent of required seating may be located seaward of the shore public walkway.

(3) Planting

Planting areas: An area equal to at least 50 percent of the area of the shore public walkway and supplemental public access area shall be planted, for zoning lots occupied by predominantly commercial or community facility uses, such area shall be equal to at least 40 percent. Where a supplemental public access area is greater than 1,875 square feet, at least 25 percent of the required planting area of the shore public walkway and supplemental public access area, combined, shall be provided as lawn. Up to 15 percent of the required planting area may be located seaward of a shore public walkway and shall be measured in plan view and not along the planted slope. When a dedicated bicycle path is provided within a supplemental public access area, a planting area with a width of at least 5 feet shall be provided between the bicycle path and any paved area for pedestrian use. For the purpose of calculating planting requirements, the area of the bicycle path may be deducted from the combined area of the shore public walkway or supplemental public access area.

Screening buffer: A screening buffer shall be provided within the shore public walkway or the supplemental public access area, running along the entire upland boundary of such area where it abuts non-publicly accessible areas of the zoning lot. The minimum width of the screening buffer shall be 10 feet. On shallow lots where the width of the shore public walkway may be reduced pursuant to Section 62-53, the width of the screening buffer may be reduced proportionally but shall not be less than four feet.

No screening buffer shall be required: adjacent to a private drive, a street or at the entrances to buildings; or for a commercial or community facility use where at least 70 percent of the area of the building façades, within a height of 10 feet, located within a distance of 15 feet from the sidewalk or waterfront public access area, is glazed with windows, transoms, or glazed portions of doors. Not less than 50 percent of the entire area of such commercial or community facility use shall be glazed with transparent materials and up to 20 percent of such area may be glazed with translucent materials.

Trees and additional planting: A minimum of one canopy tree shall be provided for every 2,000 square feet of shore public walkway and supplemental public access area. In no event may a shore public walkway have less than two canopy trees for every 100 feet of shoreline. For every 1,250 square feet of shore public walkway and supplemental public access area, one of the following must be provided: a canopy tree, an ornamental tree or a multi-stemmed equivalent, 60 square feet of planting beds, or 110 square feet of accessible lawn. Trees and additional planting areas may be located anywhere within the shore public walkway or supplemental public access area.

(4) Bicycle Parking

Bicycle racks sufficient to provide at least four bicycle parking spaces shall be provided within a waterfront public access area. Furthermore, when the combined area of the shore public walkway and supplemental public access area is greater than 8,000 square feet, two additional bicycle parking spaces shall be provided for every additional 2,000 square feet of shore public walkway or supplemental public access area. Bicycle racks shall be adjacent to a circulation path and at least 20 feet from the shoreline. Such bicycle racks may be located in public sidewalks adjacent to the zoning lot.

(5) Trash Receptacles

One trash receptacle shall be provided for every 4,000 square feet of shore public walkway and supplemental public access area, and all trash receptacles shall be located in visible and convenient locations.

2.3 Design Requirements for Public Access on Piers and Floating Structures

(1) Design Requirements for Public Access on Piers

The design requirements of this Section shall apply to waterfront public access areas on piers.

Circulation and access: At least one circulation path having a minimum clear width of 10 feet shall be provided throughout the public access area required on the pier.

Permitted obstructions: Pier public access areas may include one freestanding open or enclosed public pavilion, provided such structure does not exceed one story, is no taller than 30 feet and has an area no larger than 1,600 square feet. At least 50 percent of the perimeter wall area on all sides, up to a height of 15 feet, shall consist of clear or glazed materials which may include show windows, glazed transoms, glazed portions of doors or latticework. Such structures shall be exempt from building spacing requirements on piers, provided they maintain a spacing of at least 12 feet from other buildings and from any water edge of the pier, except that when a pier is 30 feet or less in width, a pavilion may abut one water edge.

Seating: At least one linear foot of seating is required for every 100 square feet of pier public access area.

(2) Design Requirements for Public Access on Floating Structures

The design requirements of this Section shall apply to shore public walkways provided in conjunction with as-of-right development on floating structures.

Circulation and access: A circulation path shall be provided with a minimum clear width of 10 feet. On shallow portions of zoning lots where the width of the shore public walkway may be reduced, the minimum clear width of the path may be reduced to a minimum of 6 feet when the shore public walkway is less than 16 feet.

Seating: At least one linear foot of seating is required for every 100 square feet of public access area.

Screening: Any service areas, such as that used for equipment storage or similar purposes, shall be screened from the circulation path.

2.4 Public Access Design Reference Standards

The standards of this Section, inclusive, shall be applicable to all waterfront public access areas and visual corridors. No hollow plastic material, such as PVC (polyvinyl chloride) or similar material shall be permitted in guardrails, fences, seating, trash receptacles or other similar furniture within a waterfront public access area. However, high-density polyethylene shall be permitted.

(1) Guardrails, Gates and Other Protective Barriers

Guardrails: For the purposes of this paragraph, the term "guardrail" shall refer only to fencing or similar structures provided along a bulkhead, stabilized shore or the water edges of a pier or platform. When a guardrail is provided, it shall have a maximum height of 42 inches measured from the adjoining grade level, and shall be at least 70 percent open. Guardrails may be mounted on a solid curb not higher than 6 inches.

Bollards shall be limited to the following locations: Along the bulkhead, stabilized shore or the water edges of a pier or platform. Along a zoning lot line adjacent to, and limiting access from an upland street. Along the boundaries of a roadway within an upland connection. Bollards shall not exceed 30 inches in height and shall be between six and fifteen inches in width. The top of bollards shall not consist of any sharp edges. The minimum clearance between two bollards shall be five feet.

Fences and walls, when provided, shall be limited to the following locations: Along the boundary of a waterfront public access area and an adjoining private area on the zoning lot. Around the perimeter of a playground, tot-lot or dog-run. Adjoining WD uses. Within a visual corridor. Along any grade level change of 30 inches or greater. Fences shall have a maximum height of 36 inches measured from the adjoining grade level, and be at least 70 percent open. Fences may be mounted on a solid curb not higher than 6 inches. Walls shall not exceed a height of 21 inches, and may be fully opaque. Chain link fencing or barbed or razor wire shall not be permitted.

Gates: Gates attached to fences and walls that limit physical access to waterfront public access areas from streets, public parks or other public ways, or from adjacent waterfront public access areas on adjoining zoning lots, shall comply with the provisions of this paragraph. Such gates shall be permitted only at the boundaries of waterfront public access areas and such adjacent publicly accessible areas, except that in Type 1 upland connections gates may be located at the seaward boundary of the entry area. Gates shall not intrude into any planting area. The maximum height of a gate shall be 4 feet above the adjoining grade level. Gates shall be no more than 30 percent opaque. When opened for access, 70 percent of the total width, in aggregate, of the waterfront public access area shall be free of obstructions associated with the gate, and there shall be a minimum clear distance of at least 16 feet between any two obstructions of the gate.

(2) Seating

Seating with backs: At least 50 percent of the required seating shall have backs, and at least 50 percent of such seating shall face in the general direction of the water. Seat backs shall be at least 14 inches high. Walls located adjacent to a seating surface shall not count as seat backs. All seat backs must either be contoured in form for comfort or shall be reclined from the vertical between 10 to 15 degrees.

Depth: Seating with or without backs shall have a depth of not less than 18 inches, and for seating with backs, such depth shall not be greater than 20 inches. Seating with a depth of at least 36 inches, and accessible from both sides, may be credited as double seating. When seating is provided on a planter ledge, such ledge must have a minimum depth of 22 inches.

Height: At least 75 percent of the required seating shall have a heightnot less than 16 inches nor greater than 20 inches above the level of the adjacent grade. Seating higher than 36 inches or lower than 12 inches shall not qualify toward the seating requirements. Seating may be mounted on a solid curb not higher than 6 inches.

Clearance: Seating shall be located a minimum of 22 inches from any circulation path or permitted obstruction along the accessible side of such seating, except that seating without backs may be as close to a guardrail as 12 inches.

Types of seating: In shore public walkways and supplemental public access areas, at least two of the following types of seating are required: moveable seating, fixed individual seats, fixed benches with backs, fixed benches without backs, lounging chairs and design feature seating.

Moveable seating: Moveable chairs, excluding those in open air cafés, may be credited as 18 inches of linear seating per chair; however, not more than 50 percent of required linear seating may be in moveable chairs. Moveable chairs may be placed in storage outside of the required hours of operation. All moveable chairs must have backs. Moveable chairs shall not be chained, fixed, or otherwise secured while the waterfront public access area is open to the public.

Seating steps: Seating steps shall not include any steps intended for circulation and must have a height not less than 12 inches nor greater than 30 inches and a depth not less than 18 inches.

Lounge chairs: Lounge chairs shall allow for a reclined position supporting the back as well as the legs. Lounge chairs may be credited as 36 inches of linear seating per chair.

Social seating and tables: At least 25 percent of required seating shall be social seating, consisting of seats that are placed in close proximity and at angles to one another or in facing configurations that facilitate social interaction. A minimum of 2 square feet of tables shall be required for every 3 linear feet of social seating. However, any requirement for tables that, in total, is less than square feet shall be waived, and no more than 150 square feet of tables shall be required in any site.

Shaded seating: At least 20 percent of required seating shall be shaded. Seating shall be considered shaded if it is located under a canopy tree or shade structure, or on the eastern side and within 45 feet of the trunk of a canopy tree or of a shade structure.

Seaward seating: Up to 25 percent of required seating may be located seaward of the shore public walkway provided it is designed as: A generally smooth and flat surface within a stabilized natural shoreline, in the form of rock, stone, wood or other solid material that measures at least 15 inches in width and depth and is between 12 and 30 inches high measured from the adjoining accessible surface. Seating in open air cafés or stairs shall not qualify towards seating requirements. All seating located within a planting area shall be on permeable pavement and secured for stability.

(3) Signage

The provisions of this Section shall apply to signs required in waterfront public access areas. All such signs shall be located in directly visible locations, without any obstruction at any time. Such signs shall be fully opaque, non-reflective and constructed of permanent, highly durable materials, such as metal or stone. All lettering shall be in a clear, sans-serif, non-narrow font such as Arial, Helvetica, or Verdana, solid in color with a minimum height of one-quarter inch, unless otherwise specified in this Section, and shall highly contrast with the background color.

Drawings documenting the size, format, and orientation of all required signs shall be included in the application for certification, pursuant to Section 62-80. Such drawings shall include detailed information about dimensions of the sign, lettering size, color, and materials.

Entry signage: All waterfront public access areas shall contain an entry sign mounted on a permanent structure. Such sign shall be located within five feet of the boundary of the entrance from a street, public park or other public way. Required signage shall contain:

The New York City waterfront symbol, 12 inches square in dimension, as provided in the Required Signage Symbols file at the Department of City Planning website and the New York Waterfront Symbol Standards and (published by the Department of City Planning, April 1989, and as modified from time to time).

Lettering at least one-and one-half inches in height, stating "OPEN TO PUBLIC" in bold type. Lettering at least one-half inch in height stating the approved hours of operation. Lettering at least one-half inch in height enter outside.

The International Symbol of Access for persons with physical disabilities, at least 3 inches square. The address of the property where the waterfront public access area is located. The name of the current owner and the name, phone number, and email address of the person designated to maintain the waterfront public access area.

All information required in this paragraph, shall be included on signs with a maximum dimension in one direction of 16 inches. The maximum height of a sign above the adjoining grade shall be 3 feet for a horizontal sign and 5 feet for a vertical sign. The bottom of all signs shall be at least eighteen inches above adjoining grade, except for signs angled 45 degrees or less as measured from adjacent grade.

Signage at zoning lot line: A sign shall be required to be located within five feet of any zoning lot line adjacent to another zoning lot within a shore public walkway and at a distance no greater than 5 feet from the required circulation path. All information required in this Section shall be included on signs with a maximum dimension in one direction of 16 inches. The maximum height of a sign above adjoining grade shall be 3 feet. The bottom of all signs shall be at least 18 inches above adjoining grade, except for signs angled 45 degrees or less, as measured from adjacent grade.

Other signage: Seating areas within waterfront public access areas allowed pursuant to Design Requirements for Shore Public Walkways and Supplemental Public Access Areas shall be identified by a sign with the words such sign shall be clearly visible from the waterfront public access area. In addition, such sign shall be no greater than 60 square inches, no higher than 18 inches above adjacent grade, and angled for visibility. The required sign may be freestanding or attached to a permitted amenity within the waterfront public access area. No advertising signs may be located within a waterfront public access area.

(4) Planting and Trees

Within waterfront public access areas and parking areas where planting or screening is required, the design standards of this Section shall apply. A detailed landscape plan prepared by a registered landscape architect shall be submitted to the Department of Parks and Recreation prior to seeking certification by the Chairperson of the City Planning Commission. Such plans shall include plants suited for waterfront conditions and include a diversity of species with emphasis on native plants, salt tolerance and the facilitation of sustainable wildlife habitats, where appropriate. No species listed on quarantine or as a host species for any disease listed by the Department of Parks and Recreation at the time of application shall be included. All landscaped areas shall contain a built-in irrigation system or contain hose bibs within 100 feet of all planting areas.

Single tree pits: A single tree pit shall have a minimum dimension of 5 feet with a minimum area of 30 square feet and a minimum depth of 3 feet, 6 inches. Only tree pits planted with ground cover shall count towards meeting a minimum planting area requirement.

Continuous tree pits: A continuous tree pit is a planting area containing two or more trees. Continuous tree pits shall have a minimum width of 5 feet and a minimum depth of 3 feet, 6 inches, and a length as required to meet a minimum of 5 feet from the trunk of the tree to the end of the tree pit.

Planting beds: Planting beds for turf grass or groundcovers shall have minimum dimensions of 2 feet in any direction and a minimum depth of 2 feet. Planting beds for shrubs shall have minimum dimensions of 3 feet by 3 feet for each shrub and a minimum depth of 2 feet, 6 inches. Planting beds containing trees shall have a minimum dimension of 5 feet and a minimum area of 30 square feet for each tree, with a minimum depth of 3 feet, 6 inches. Trees, shrubs, or groundcovers may be combined in a single planting bed only if such bed meets the minimum depth required for the largest plant.

Berms: A "berm" is a planting area with sloped grade stabilized primarily by plant materials rather than retaining walls or other similar built structures. A berm shall comply with the dimensional standards for a planting bed except that the height from the adjacent grade to the top of the berm shall not exceed 60 inches.

Lawns: A "lawn" is an area planted with turf grass having a minimum soil depth of 2 feet, 6 inches. Along at least 60 percent of the perimeter, a lawn shall have a grade level within six inches of the adjacent grade providing unobstructed pedestrian access. Any required lawn shall have a minimum area of 500 square feet and no dimension less than 18 feet.

Screening: Screening is intended to create a landscaped buffer between the waterfront public access areas and adjoining non-public uses to protect the privacy or minimize the visual impact of blank walls, equipment, loading and parking areas or similar conditions.

Screening buffers: Screening buffers required pursuant Design Requirements for Shore Public Walkways and Supplemental Public Access Areas shall consist of densely planted shrubs or multi-stemmed screening plants, with at least 50 percent being evergreen species. Shrubs shall have a height of at least four feet at the time of planting.

Blank walls and service areas: Blank walls higher than four feet measured from an adjacent grade level and service areas anywhere within a waterfront public access area shall be screened with any combination of evergreen trees, vines or espaliered trees or shrubs, and an architectural treatment such as a pergola, stone rustication, grills, or sculptural features.

Parking garage screening: Open parking areas on any zoning lot fronting on an upland connection or street on any waterfront block, notwithstanding the use on such lot, shall require screening pursuant to Perimeter landscaping. Plants shall be at least four feet high at the time of planting and 50 percent of them shall be evergreen shrubs.

Trees: At time of planting, canopy trees shall be a minimum of three inches caliper and ornamental trees shall be a minimum of two inches caliper. Granite or cast concrete block pavers with a minimum four inch depth shall be installed in accordance with New York City Department of Parks and Recreation (DPR) standards for street trees. A grate shall be installed over the root zone, supported at its edges and set flush with the adjacent pavement for pedestrian safety, in accordance with DPR standards for street trees for grate size. The root zone shall be surrounded with barrier hedge planting.

(5) Paving

Within required circulation paths: Unit pavers constituted of stone, concrete, granite, asphalt, or a mix of these materials with other aggregates. Concrete, prefabricated, poured, or permeable. Wood planks for boardwalk or decking, except that tropical hardwood shall not be permitted. Polyethylene, wood composite plastic, or fiber-reinforced plastic.

Other than within required circulation paths: Blocks such as Belgian blocks, cobble stones, concrete cobbles, or Euro cobble. Gravel, loose, installed over a solid surface or glued with resin. Wood chips or other similar material. Metal grating, limited to locations that require drainage and for platforms. Asphalt, impermeable or porous, which may be imprinted with thermoplastic patterns.

(6) Bicycle Racks

Each bicycle rack shall allow for the bicycle frame and one wheel to be locked to the rack. If bicycles can be locked to each side of the rack, each side may be counted as a required space. 30 inches of maneuverable space shall be provided between parallel bicycle racks and an 8 foot wide aisle shall be provided between bicycle rack areas.

(7) Trash Receptacles

Trash receptacles shall be placed within 50 feet of a seating area, have a minimum capacity of 25 gallons and have either top openings that measure at least 12 inches wide or side openings that inscribe a rectangle measuring at least 12 inches wide and 6 inches high. Trash receptacles shall be able to use standard bags used to collect trash.

References
1. City of Seattle, Guiding Principles for Waterfront Design
2. New York City Department of City Planning, Zoning Resolution—Design Requirments For Waterfront Public Access Areas

Mulini Beach

Location: Rovinj, Croatia
Area: 13,515m²
Completion Date: 2014
Landscape Design: Luka Brnić, Studio 3LHD
Photography: Joao Morgado
Client: Maistra d.d.

Mulini Beach is located in an attractive area of Rovinj, on the exit from the central part of the city and in the continuation of the promenade, in front of hotels Monte Mulini, Lone, and Eden, wrapped in a rich green public park and green forest protective areas.

It is an extension of the city's public area and the promenade whose primary function is to connect the city of Rovinj and park Punta Corrente.

An extremely important factor in the design of the beach was the relationship to existing terrain. With regard to the specific environment that is completely different depending on the time of day (the sea level varies in approximately 80 cm) due to the influence of the tides the design was dependent on the sea as a variable element, the sea has significantly influenced the creative decisions during the design process.

That is why the entire area of the beach is divided into two zones: a stretch from the marina to the beach pavilion that is greatly influenced by the waves, and a much calmer bay with a pebble beach. The first zone is designed as a natural topography, with lots of fractured surfaces for sunbathing and relatively sparse vegetation. The calmer Lone bay is formed as a pebble beach with lush vegetation that gently slopes into the sea.

Site Plan With the Beach and the Surrounding Hotels

Mulini Beach Bar, a beach facility with a large bar, locker rooms, showers, toilets and an information desk is located in the center of the zone. In the evening, the beach bar turns into a more intimate lounge with a cozy atmosphere by the sea. It is designed as a pavilion with a floating pergola roof – a steel structure that rests on 6 points, whose final shape was determined by an analysis of the sun movement through the summer months. The pergola, weighing 20 tons, has a span of 30m in length. It is constructed from steel sheets 8mm and 20mm thick, and has a total height of 20cm. The bar can be closed with a sliding wall that is stored inside a storage room during the day. The sliding wall is hung from the pergola construction. The plateau in front of the bar is equipped with infrastructure that allows small concerts and entertainment.

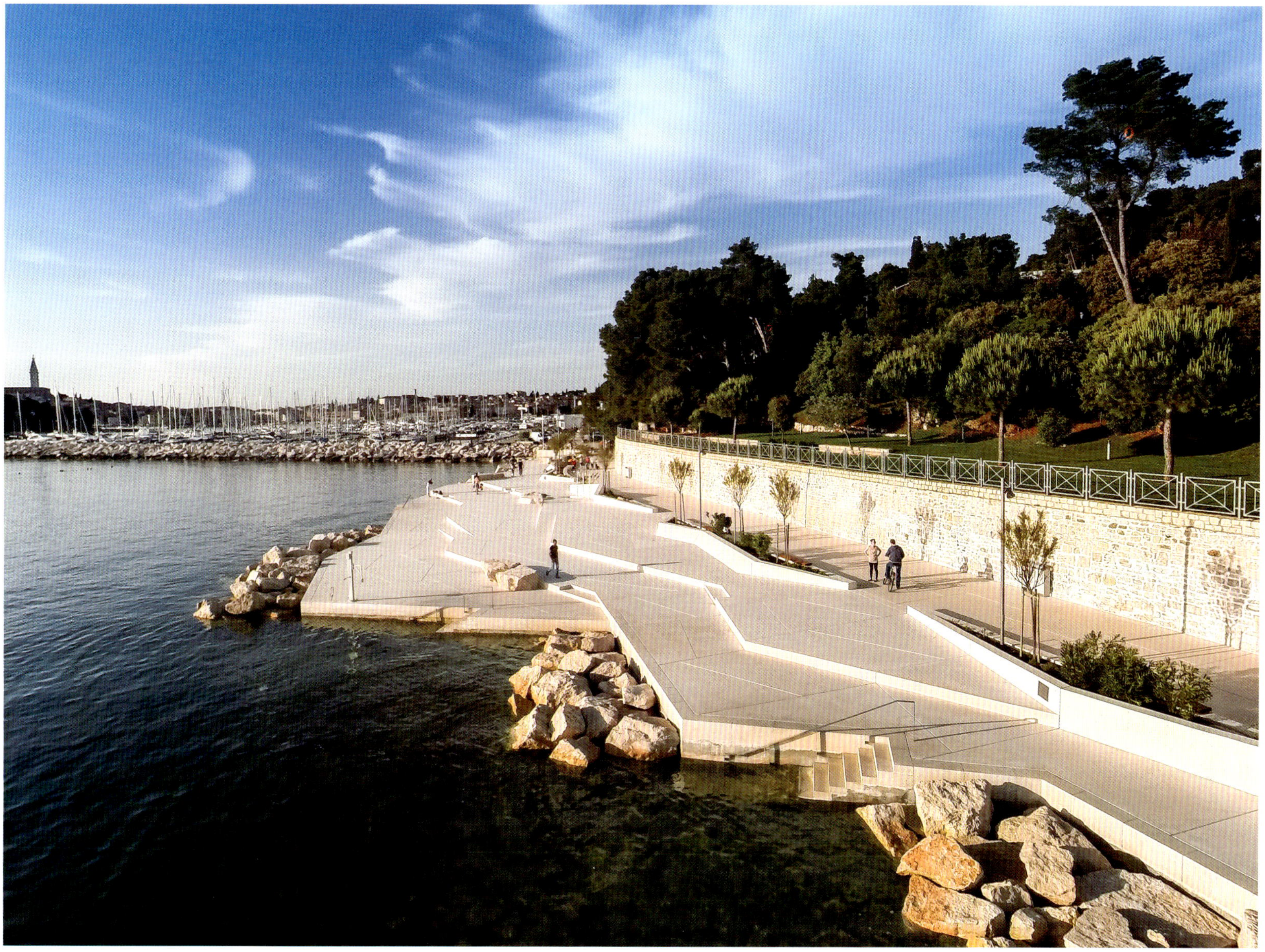

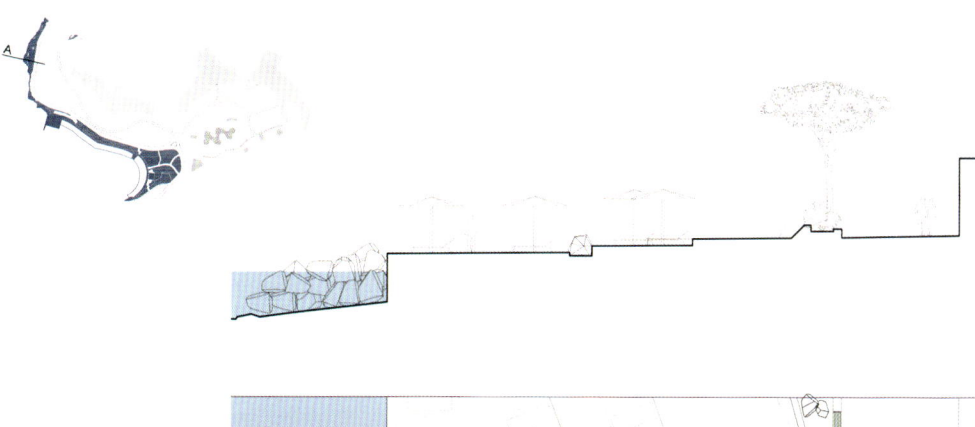

Fractured sunbathing surfaces and sparse vegetation.

m 1 2 5 10

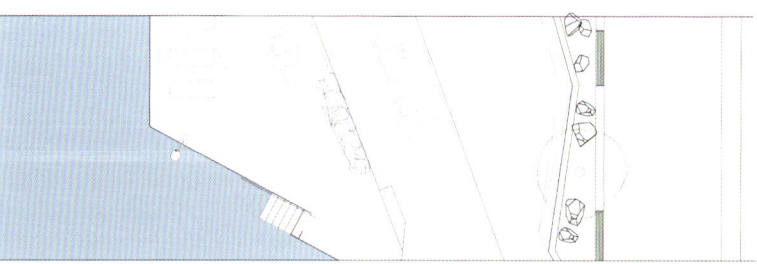

Section A

The first zone of the beach, with fractured sunbathing surfaces and sparse vegetation.

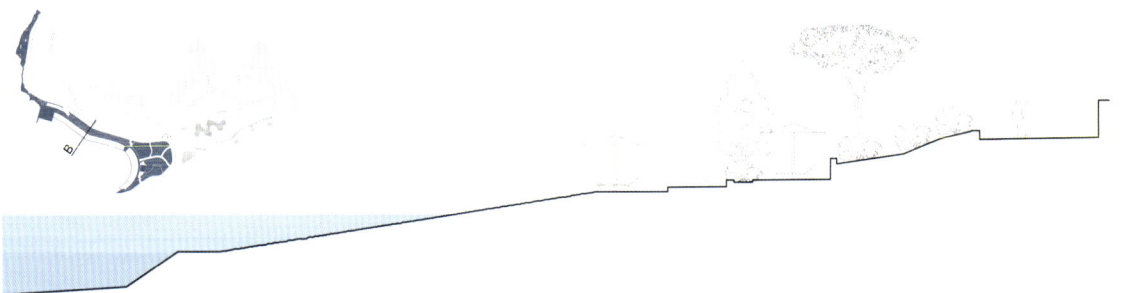

Calmer Lone Bay formed as a pebble beach.

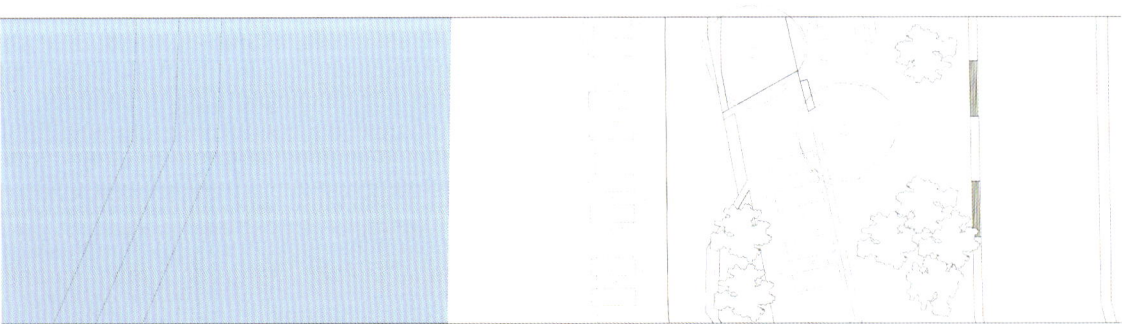

Section B
Calmer pebble beach with vegetation and sunbathing chairs.

m 1 2 5 10

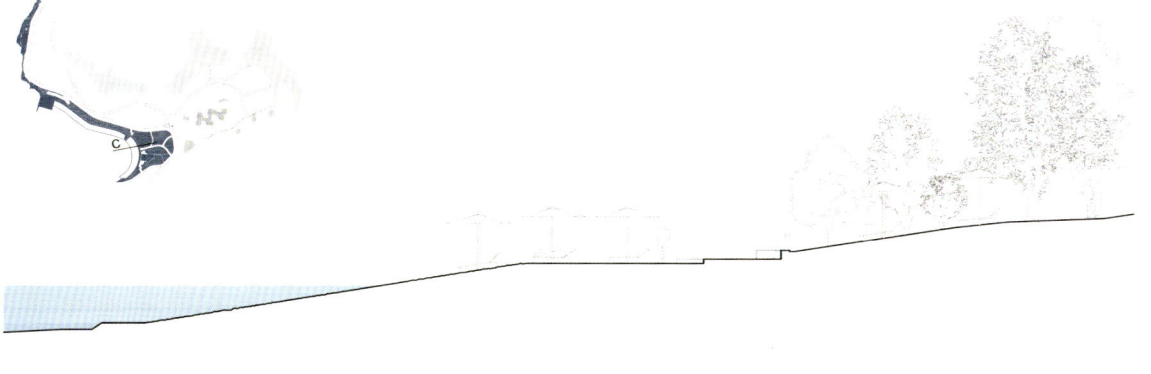

View of the beach and Hotel Lone in the background.

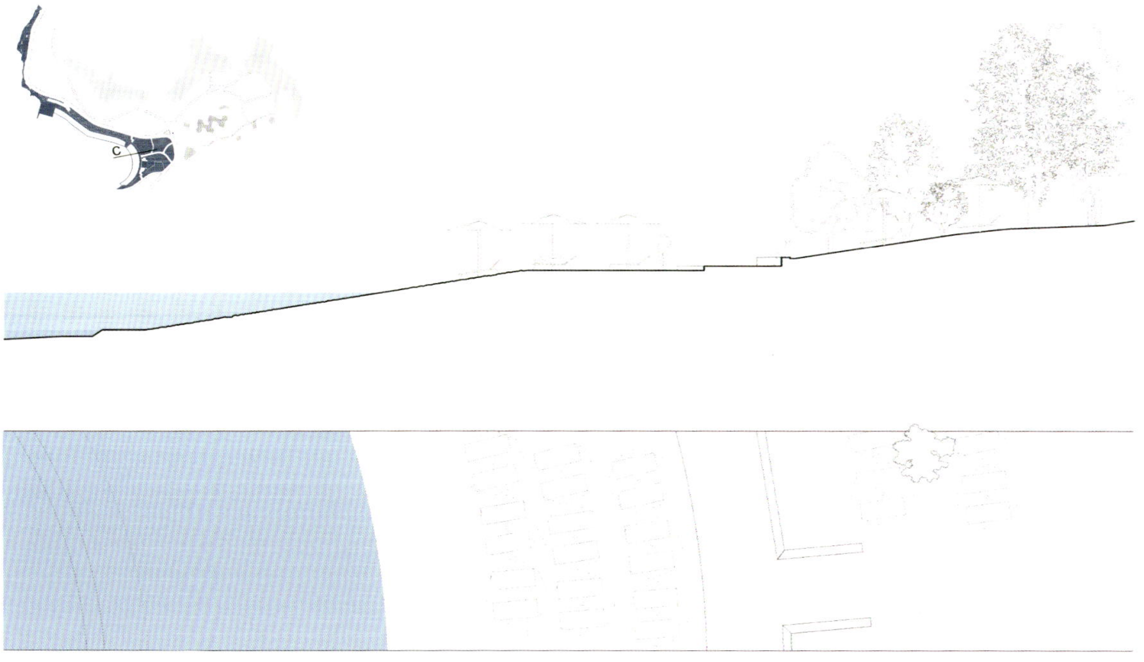

Section C
Sunbathing pebble beach.

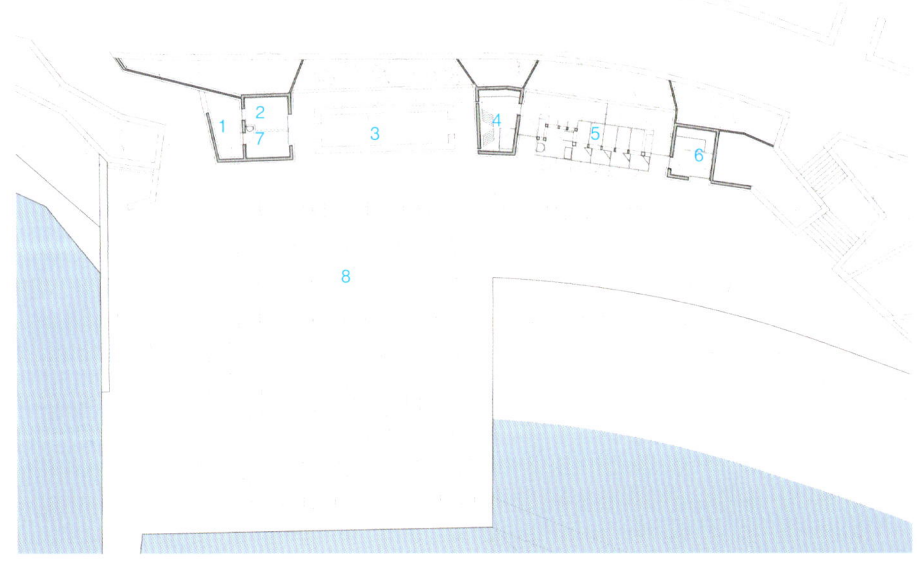

Areal view of the calmer part of the Lone Bay.

Siteplan

1. Service Entry
2. Drink Storage
3. Café
4. Storage
5. Toilet / Communication
6. Reception
7. Sandwich and Salad Preparation
8. "Mulini Beach" Plateau

Aerial view of the Mulini Beach Bar and the plateau in front of it.

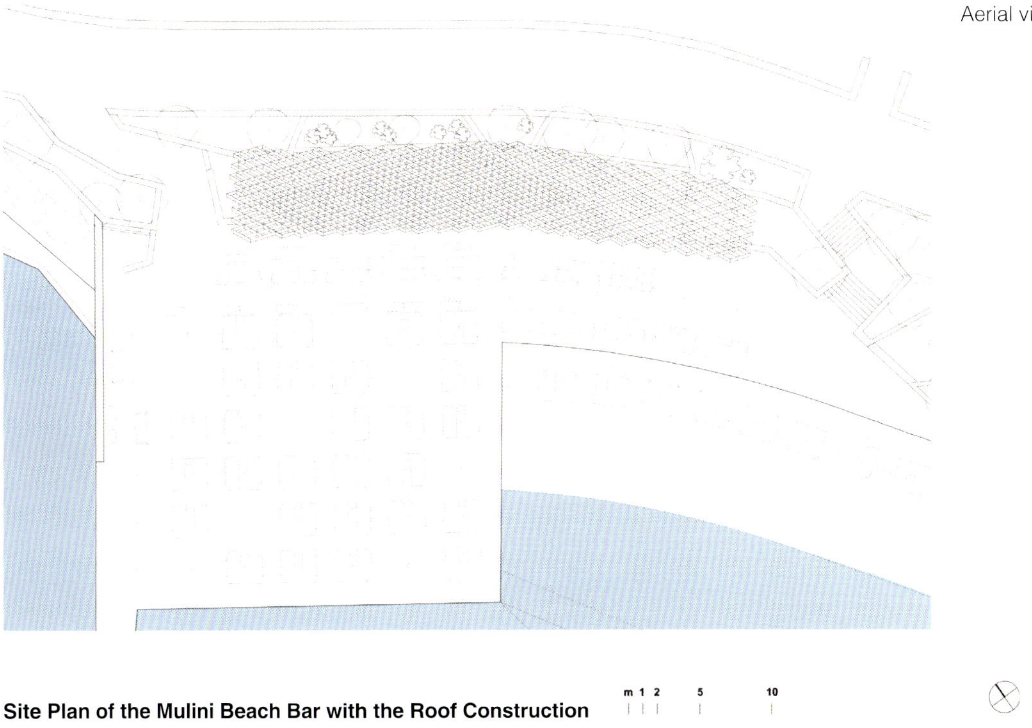

Site Plan of the Mulini Beach Bar with the Roof Construction

Mulini Beach Bar and terrace.

Pavilion / Beach Bar Axonometry

1. Steel Construction Pergola
2. Bar
3. Toilet, Changing Rooms
4. Service Area
5. Existing Promenade Wall
6. Silding Wall Storage Room

Top left: Beach bar detail.
Top right: Changing rooms on the beach.

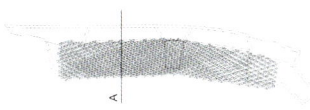

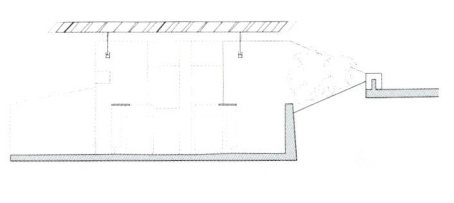

Beach Bar Sections A

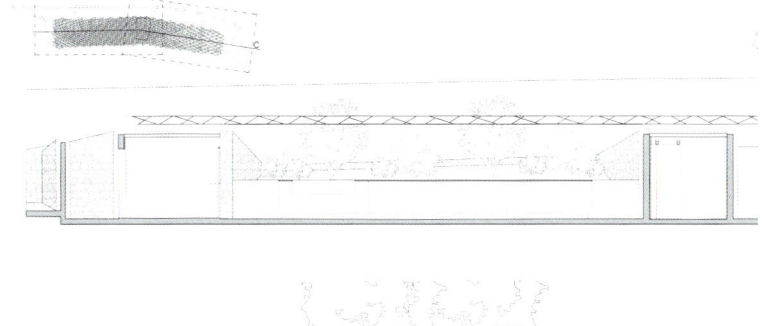

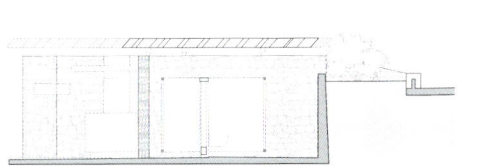

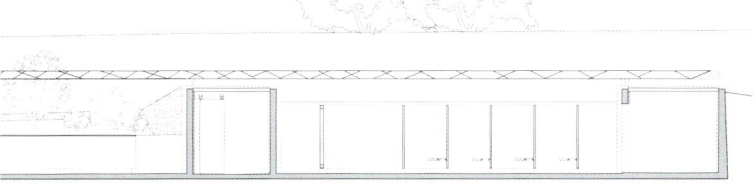

Beach Bar Sections B

Beach Bar Section C

Top: Aerial view of the fractured sunbathing area, with the view of the bay.

Bottom: Lush vegetation and sunbathing area.

Opposite top: Beach bar by night.

Opposite bottom: View of the beach bar roof construction from the promenade.

Aalborg Waterfront - Linking Port & City

Location: Aalborg, Denmark
Area: 170,000 m²
Completion Date: 2012
Landscape Design: C. F. Møller Architects, Vibeke Rønnow Landscape Architects
Photography: Helene Hoyer Mikkelsen, Vibeke Ronnow
Client: Aalborg Municipality
Award: 2014 Civic Trust Award
2013 Nordic Green Space
2011 Finalist for the Sustainable Concrete Award
2010 The Danish construction industry's honorary award
2010 Aalborg Municipality Architecture Award
2004 1st prize in architectural competition

The master plan for Aalborg Waterfront links the city's medieval centre with the adjacent fjord, which has previously been difficult for citizens to access due to the industrial harbor and the associated heavy traffic. By tying in with the openings in the urban fabric, a new relationship between city and fjord is created, and what was formerly a hinterland is turned into a new, highly attractive front.

For All Residents

The adjacent flower gardens are a calm, slightly sunken green space with a dense planting of trees and flowers. A lush, colorful oasis for all ages, primarily designed for quiet pursuits and as a recreational space for Aalborg's new floating harbor pool, which is located along the waterfront, next to "Elbjørn" – a former ice-breaker converted into a floating restaurant / workshop.

The gardens are divided by wide tali-wood decking areas, which along the harbor promenade turn into broad south-facing seating areas. To shield against the winds from Limfjorden, the gardens

Masterplan-updated

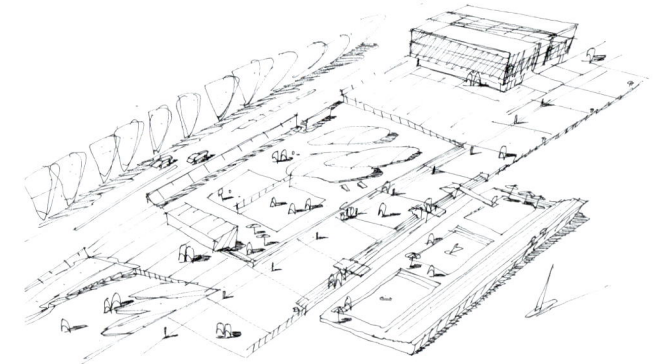
Sketch

The playground of the waterfront area.

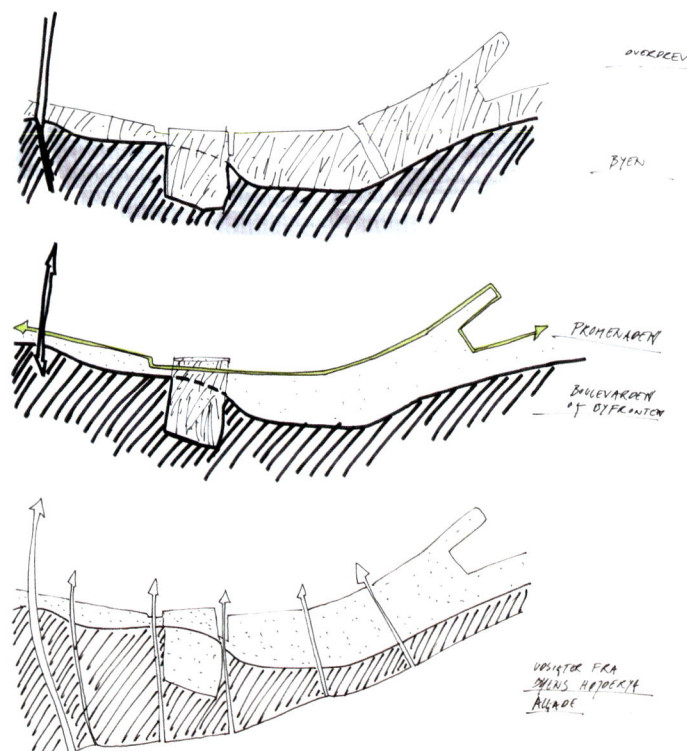

Masterplan Concept Sketch

have been sunken 60cm, and the gardens are furthermore shielded from the Strandvejen Boulevard by a long continuous bastion in smooth, white concrete, also serving as seating.

Facilities for Children

The westernmost part of the park, by Limfjord bridge, is a café garden and activity area. The City of Aalborg shows great consideration when integrating facilities for both children and young people on the waterfront. The café garden is surrounded by eateries and offers an unconventional play park with soft curved grass mounds, rubber banks, and polished stainless steel play components, small trees, and unusual lighting.

At the eastern end of the promenade, the Utzon Park frames the new exhibition centre on Aalborg's waterfront named the Utzon Centre. It is furnished with the unique concrete benches originally designed for the Sydney Opera House by Jørn Utzon. Utzon was fascinated by nature, and his works are inspired by nature's organic shapes. The park's cherry trees on a bed of spring flowers and the simple, sprawling lawn are inspired by his architectural ideas, which are also expressed in his soft, sculptural furniture design produced by Escofet.

Above: The edge of waterfront.
Opposite: The steps of the waterfront edge.

Phase Two Sketch

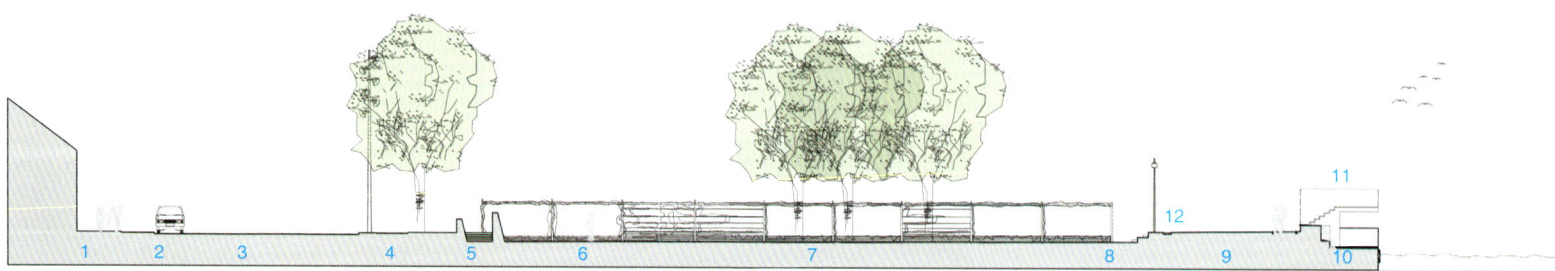

Section Urban Garden

1. Sidewalk
2. Carriageway
3. Traffic island
4. Patterned sidewalk
5. Bastion / stairs
6. Wood / steel trellis
7. Sunken park
8. Wood steps
9. Asphalt / historic rail tracks
10. Sitting steps
11. Lookout
12. Wate rill

Above: Stairs of the waterfront.
Opposite top: Flower bed.
Opposite middle: Play area.

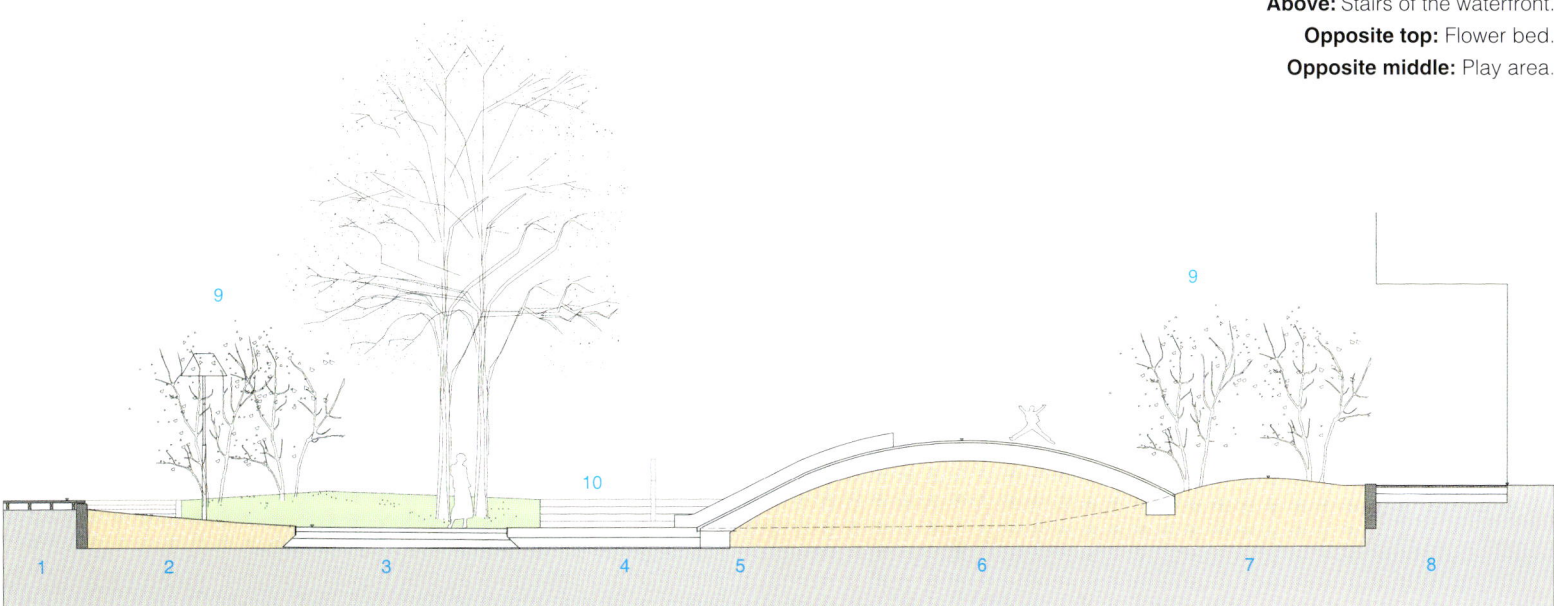

Cross-Section Playground Jomfgu Ane Park

1. Wooden deck
2. Green incline
3. Light gravel
4. Cushioning layer
5. Polished steel slide
6. Play-hill (porous re-cycled plastic paving)
7. Green incline
8. Slate sidewalk
9. Juneberry plantings
10. Wood steps

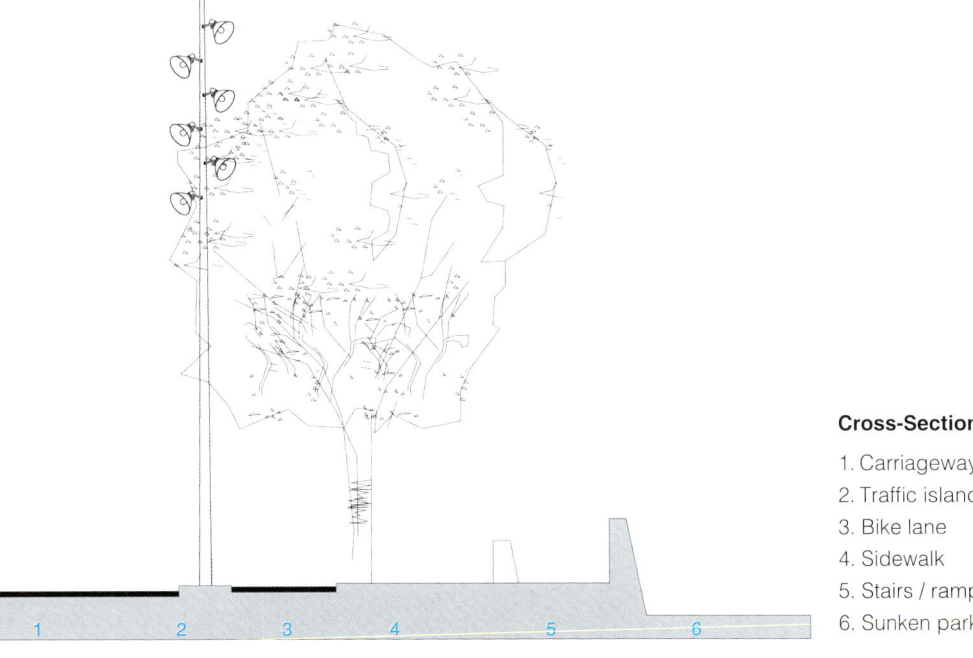

Opposite: Road pavement in pattern type.

Cross-Section Bastion

1. Carriageway
2. Traffic island
3. Bike lane
4. Sidewalk
5. Stairs / ramp
6. Sunken park

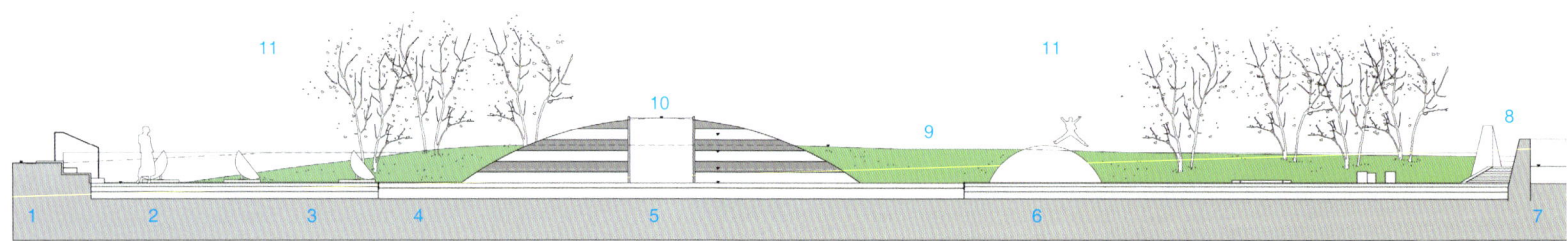

Section Playground Jomfru Ane Park

1. Water rill
2. Wooden steps
3. Light gravel
4. Cushioning layer
5. Play-hill (porous re-cycled plastic paving)
6. Polished steel sphere
7. Concrete bastion
8. Ramp
9. Green incline
10. Polished steel slide
11. Juneberry plantings

Opposite top: The small garden in front of the buildings.
Top: The pavilion in the garden is a place for people to rest.

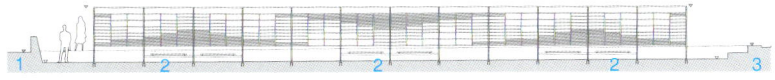

Section Urban Gardens Trellis

1. Concrete bastion
2. Seats
3. Wood steps

Above: The square along the road.
Opposite: The rest place in the garden with plenty of plants.

Planting Scheme

Anglet South Coastline

Location: Anglet, France
Area: 38,000m²
Completion Date: 2013
Landscape Design: Debarre Duplantier Associés Architecture & Paysage, Anton Y. Olano lighting designer
Photography: Arthur Péquin and Yohan Zerdoun
Client: City of Anglet

Meeting point between the high mountains of the Pyrenees and the vast expanse of the Landes forest, the southern coast of Anglet combines exceptional geography in a premium urban situation: it is the true gateway to the city from its chic neighbor Biarritz.

The singularities of this site are reflected in the project: transposition of the lithography of rocks, chunks of cliffs landed on a lawn, mirror effect and interaction between vegetal and mineral influences, organization of traffic in curtains to magnify an unusual scenery: an Atlantic panorama from the hilly Spanish coast to the northern sand beaches.

The esplanade Yves Brunaud, a remarkable gateway to the city.

On the upper part, a cantilever as a gateway to the city provides this great panorama. As a response to the ocean, a water-table and a garden mark the entrance to the city and separate the promenade and bike path from the traffic. Thus, relying on a green curtain, attention will be given to the panorama.

Getting closer: mountains and sand come together to offer us a dramatic panorama.

The site reflects the character of the sandy beaches of the north reaching the lower part of the site while mountains rocks are prevailing in the upper part. To celebrate the event, the global aspect of the cliffs are translated on the ground of the upper part.

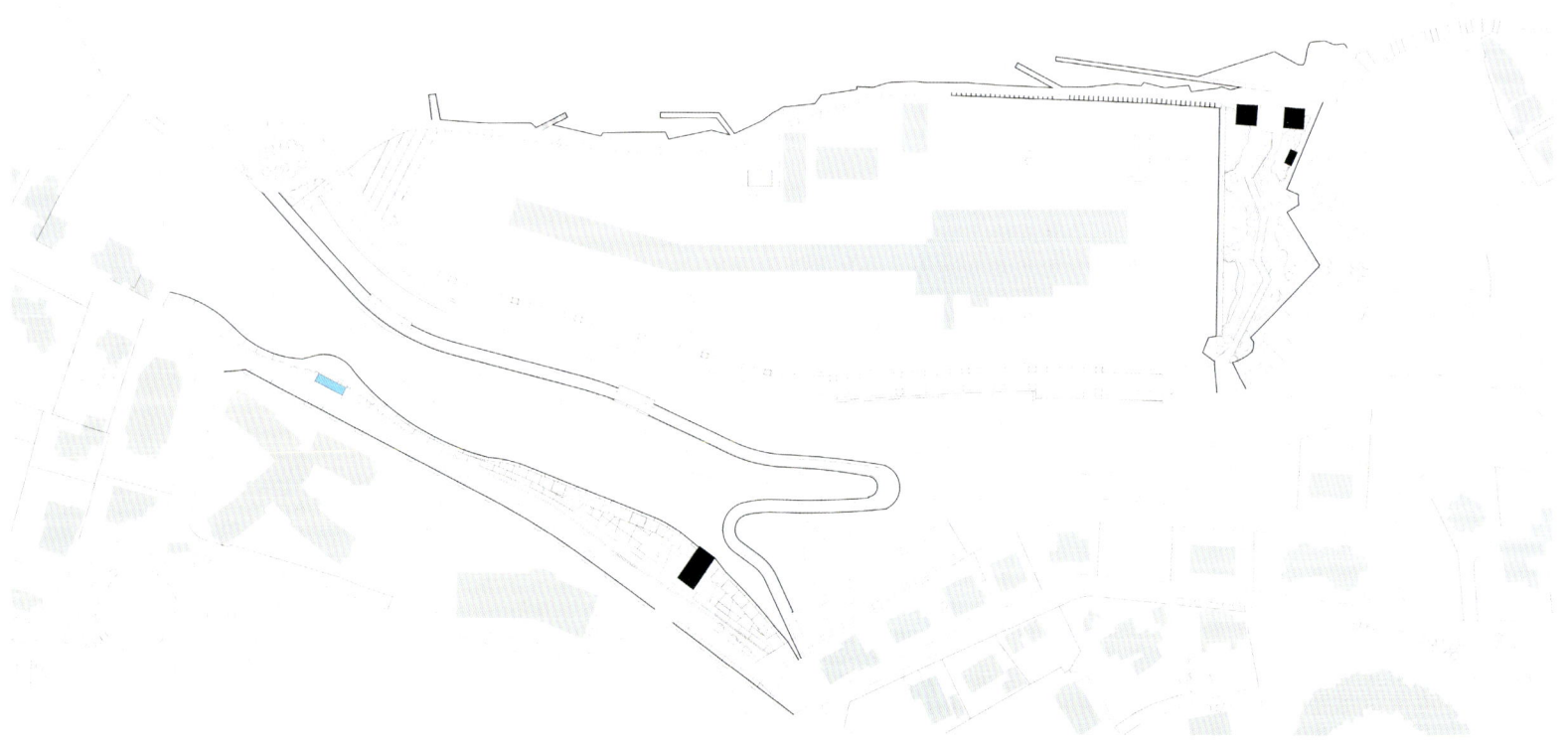

Nightime view on to the water.

Plan

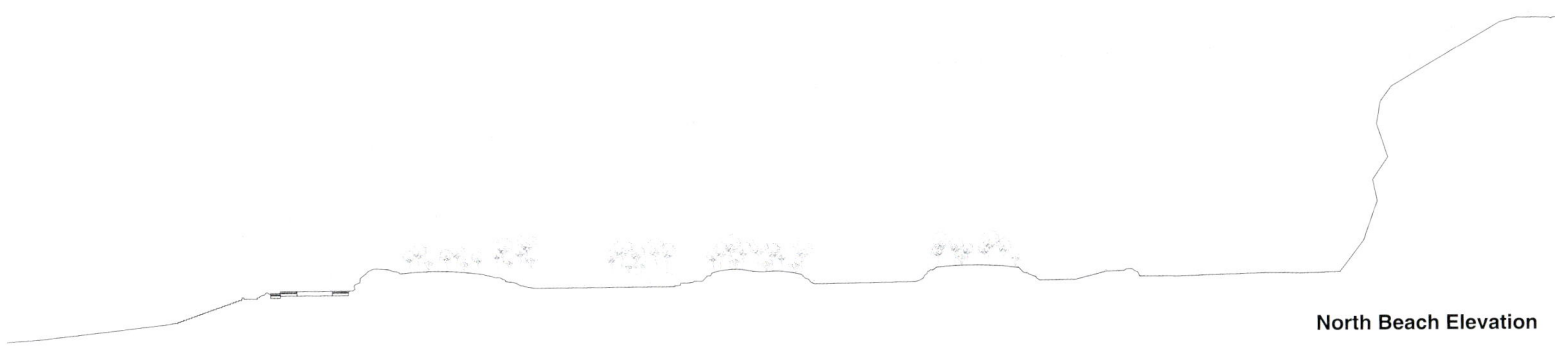

View from the Yves Brunaud esplanade.

North Beach Elevation

Similarly, big blocks of rocks are laying onto the lawn of the lower part to organize the entrance to the beach and create diverse scales of intimacy in this large landscape. The overlap of the two worlds — mountains and sand — is realized at the foot of the cliff, around the VVF.

Top: Daytime view on to the water.
Bottom: Close-up of the pergola.
Opposite: The wooded dunes.

Plan and Elevation of the Pergola

Top: Close-up of the railing, Yves Brunaud esplanade.

Opposite top: The water installation, Yves Brunaud esplanade.

Opposite bottom: The benches of the eplanade.

Sea Elevation

South Beach Elevation

191

Harbour Bath and Blue Base

Location: Faaborg, Denmark
Area: 2,100m²
Completion Date: 2014
Architeture Design: JDS / JULIEN DE SMEDT ARCHITECTS, KLAR
Photography: Julien Lanoo, JDS Architects, Mette Krull
Client: Faaborg Kommune

The new Faaborg Harbor Bath and Blue Base at the southern end of Fyn, is based on the idea of bathing in the sea and close to the elements. Waterfront landscape design is one of the important contents of landscape design: people are born with hydrophilia, especially children like playing with water. The concept of the bath is based on the idea of creating an open sea bathing area with piers branching out seawards creating swimming areas between them.

The various functions define every pier in the bath. This creates a "finger plan" with open basins between four baths bridges of different width and length, where each bridge offers a new way to get in the water and in which each pool has a specific use. The wooden piers form ramps, stairs, sitting opportunities, and small pools for children. The Harbour Bath has changing rooms, a sauna and a 300m² meeting point for boat tourism on land.

The Harbor Bath offers a wide range of different activities during the whole year: children's pool, jumping tower, row swimming, winter bathing, kayak club house, sauna, kayak storage, workshop, and changing rooms. But it functions as well as an urban space and city landscape with all different kinds of edges, ramps, stairs, and plateaus, where people can move around, play, sunbathe or just enjoy the close connection to the sea.

Competition Rendering

Competition Rendering Aerial View

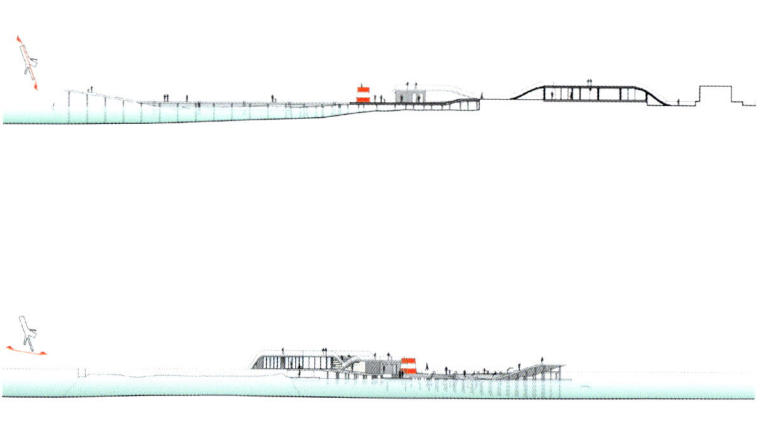

Site Plan

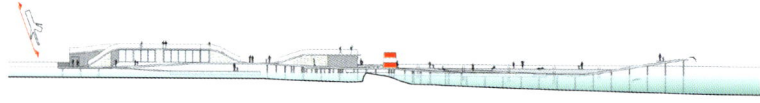

Sections

All functions and zones are connected by ramps and stairs, which guarantee accessibility for handicapped people.

The Faaborg Harbour Bath will give the town of Faaborg a new public water space which will attract visitors and invite the locals to swim and enjoy water sports.

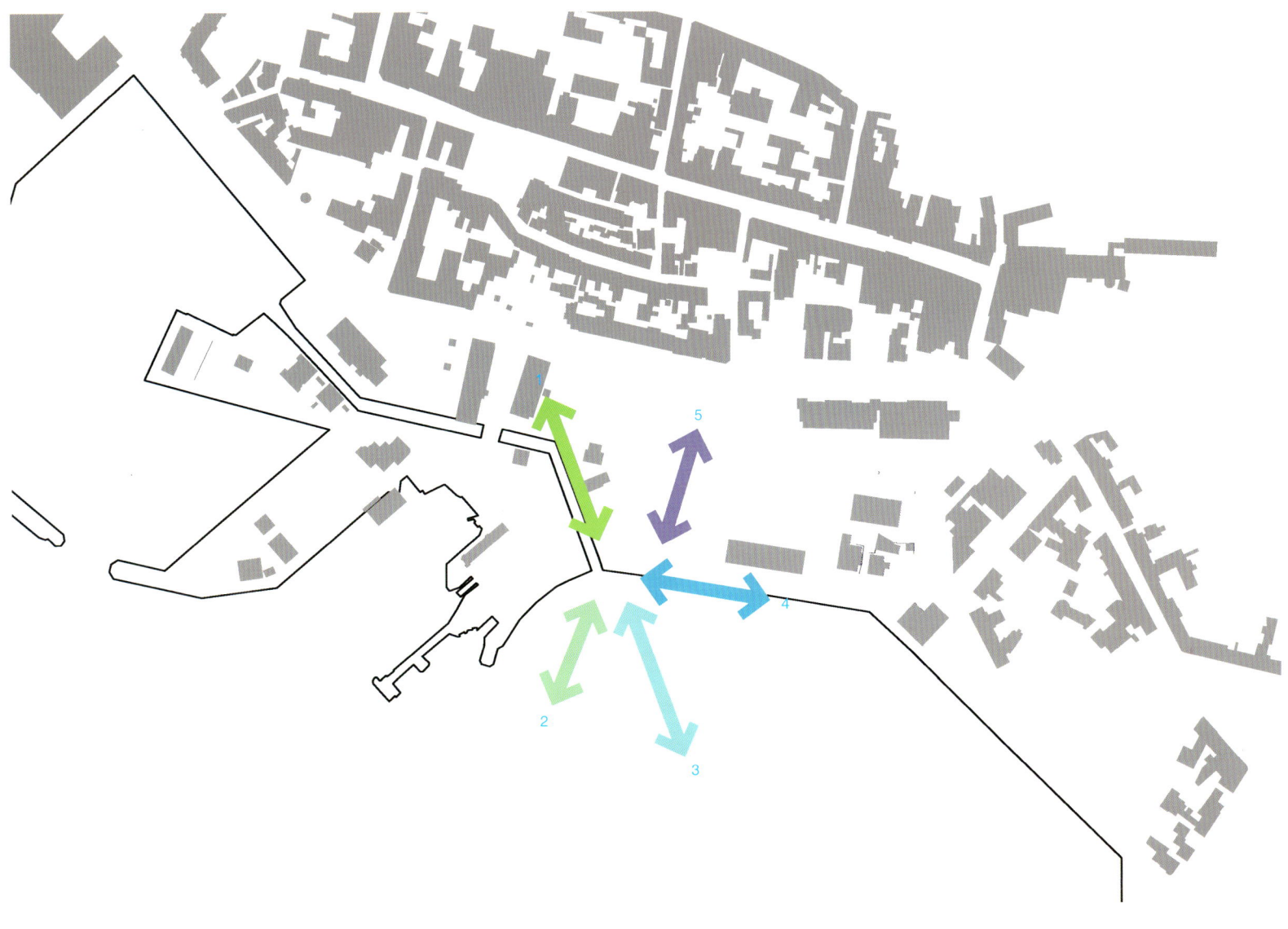

Connection Diagram
1. Town
2. Maritime sport
3. Bathing
4. Park
5. Culture

View from jumping tower to sauna.

Top: Water playground.
Opposite top: Children swimming.
Opposite bottom: Men kayaking.

Pools   Directions of Bathing Piers

198

Kayak pier and jumping tower

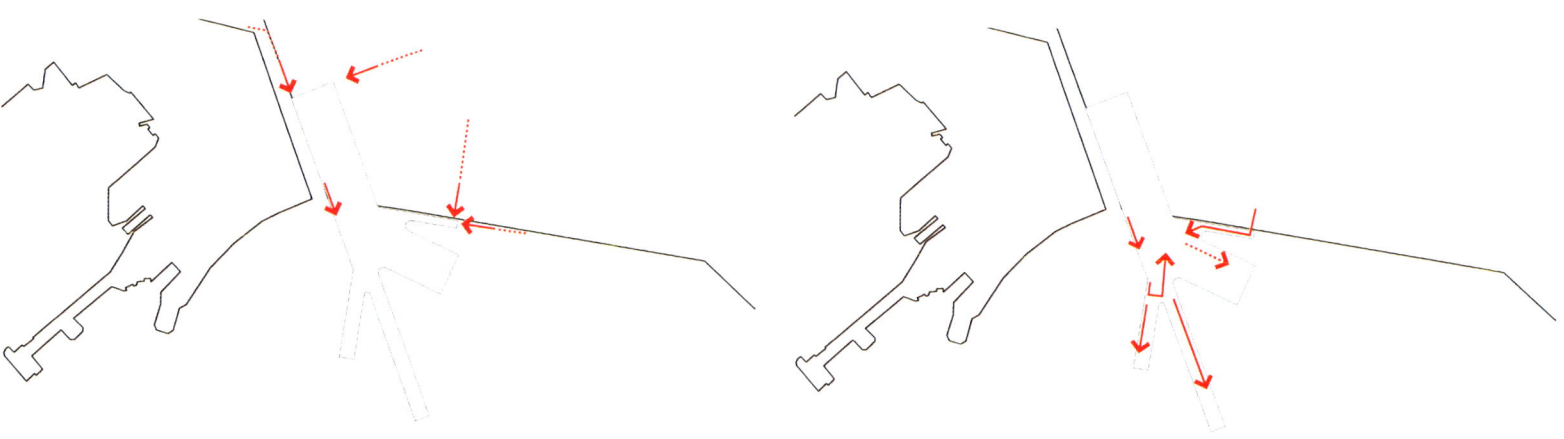

General Access **Handicap Accessibility**

Sauna building accessible roof

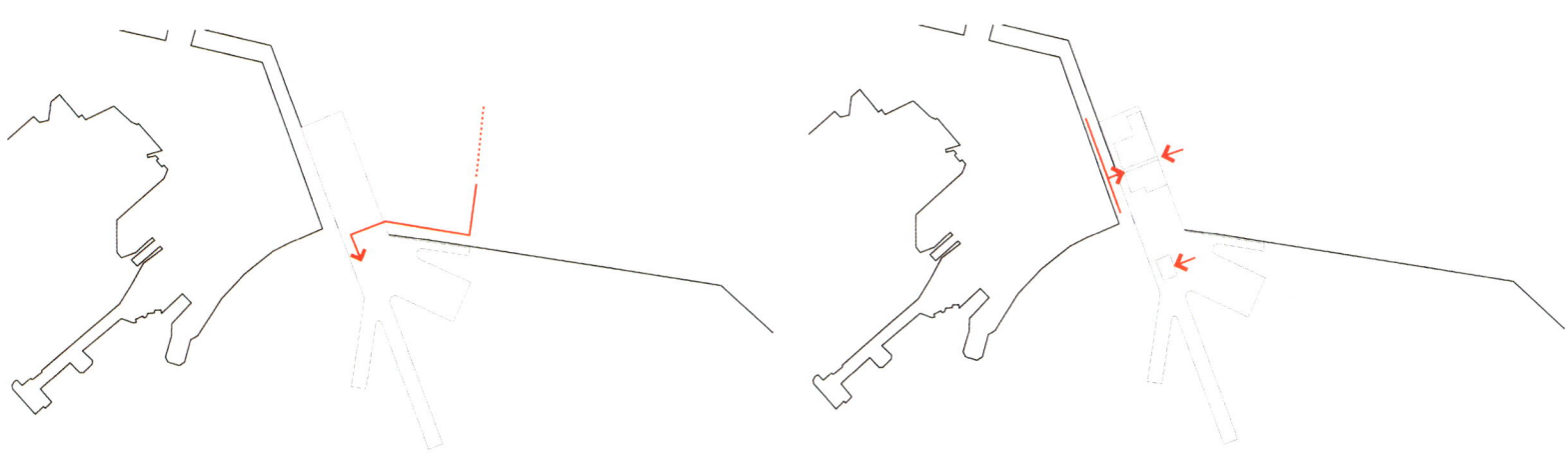

Ambulance Passage   **Pavilion Entrance**

Kid's pool

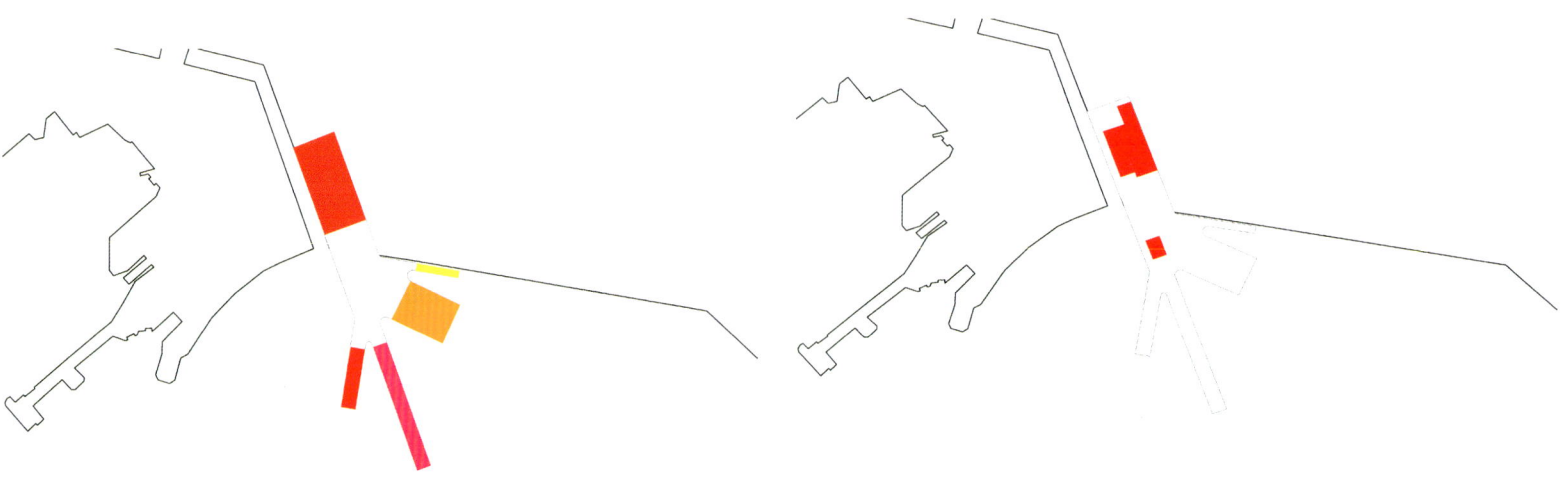

Programmatic Distribution   **Pavilions**

Top: Kayak storage.
Bottom: View from car park.

Lands End Lookout Visitors Center

Location: San Francisco, USA
Area: 1,646 m²
Completion Date: 2012
Landscape Design: SURFACEDESIGN INC.
Photography: SURFACEDESIGN INC.
Client: Golden Gate National Parks Conservancy
Awards: Cultural Landscape Foundation Award Golden Gate Plaza and Lands' End Lookout 2012

The Lands End Lookout is the newest visitor centre in the Golden Gate National Recreation Area. The landscape design for the site protects the beautiful and rugged coastline of San Francisco, while making it more visible and accessible to all visitors. Home to a unique combination of outdoor exhibits, view terraces and gathering spaces, the Lands End Lookout recounts the many stories of Lands End and the Sutro Baths and provides an improved visitor experience to the countless people who visit every year.

Many visitors to the Lookout arrive along the wild and rocky Coastal Trail, which traverses the cliffs stretching from Baker Beach to Lands End. Along the way, hikers pass hillsides of cypress and wildflowers, taking in views of old shipwrecks and the epic ruins of the Sutro Baths.

The Lookout is designed to frame the spectacular view to the ocean and ruins of the baths below. The building and its related outdoor spaces yield to the natural landscape, allowing it to be the main focus while remaining firmly rooted to the rugged edge of the Pacific. The new landscape design and the architecture blend seamlessly with the surrounding landscape. The shifting concrete wall planes of the Lookout building stretch out to embrace the dune-scape, expressing the evolution of the site and its dynamic natural environment. The Lookout also provides a forum for outdoor exhibits and displays of artifacts.

Top: View to Sutro Baths and the Pacific ocean on the left, while the visitors center sits atop the rugged bluff on the right, all surrounded by the coastal dunescape.

Opposite top: Lands End visitors center plaza. Wooden seat walls are made from reclaimed wood from felled Monterey Cypress.

Opposite middle: Repurposed lion statues from Mayor Sutro's estate.

Opposite bottom: Another view of visitors center plaza, with re-purposed stag statue as a centerpiece..

Materials used in construction of the outdoor spaces are rustic, echoing the constant wear and erosion caused by sea winds. Vertically positioned timber members, named "dune screens" mark the movement of shifting sand while serving as guideposts for visitors.

A Unique Environment

As a main entry to the Sutro Baths historic site and as a trailhead for the Coastal Trail, the Lookout affords visitors a heightened experience of San Francisco's distinctive coastal environment. The combination of the site's unique ecology, (which includes a rare confluence of fresh and brackish water), the drama of the topography, and the challenges of building and creating outdoor spaces on the face of a cliff make this a treasured place in the San Francisco landscape.

Interpretive Landscape Elements

Consistent with the National Park Service's mission to educate the public about the cultural resources and the natural history of the park, Surfacedesign integrated a program of outdoor artifacts and interpretive elements into the gardens and courtyard of the Lookout. These elements are designed to heighten a visitor's appreciation of the natural surroundings and their understanding of the specific history of the site. At the end of the 19th century, Adolph Sutro, the 24th Mayor of San Francisco, owned nearly a tenth of all the land in the city and he was responsible for building the Victorian Cliff House castle and Sutro Baths at the

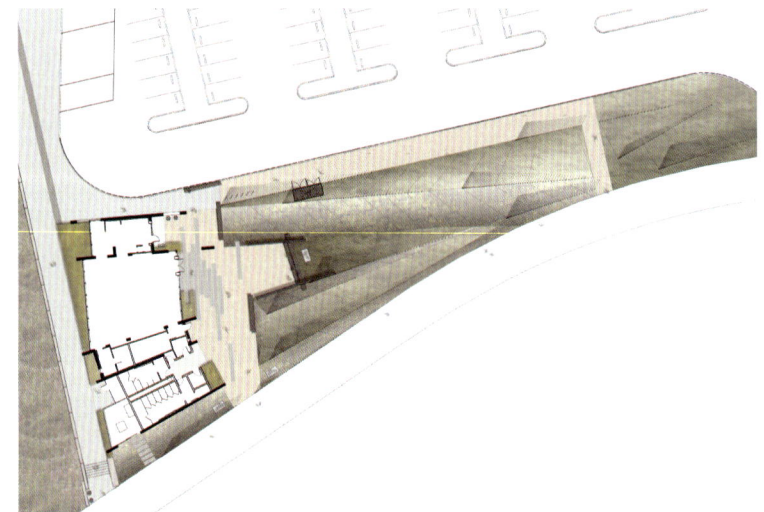

Site Plan

foot of his estate. He is today perhaps best remembered for the various San Francisco lands and landmarks that bear his name. Acknowledging the indelible mark he left on the site, remnants of the cliff-top estate he built for himself at Lands End have been integrated into the gardens and courtyard of the Lookout.

Once a windswept wilderness of desolate, forbidding sand dunes, the natural environment today is at the fringe of the City's expanded western residential neighbourhoods. The form of the new building and its placement on a series of landforms planted with native grasses are meant to recall the memory of coastal dunes and the preexisting ecology of the site.

Limited Resources

Surface design worked with a limited set of building and plant materials to maximize economy and sustainability. All of the plants used on the lookout site were harvested from a specific local watershed and cultivated in nearby nurseries by local native plant growers. Even the sand mixture used for planting was locally sourced from construction sites to ensure the plants would establish themselves in the fragile ecology. Wood used for benches and to create the dune screens was harvested from Monterey Cypress found in the park. On site trees at the end of their natural life spans were culled as part of planned periodic site maintenance. The trees have been replaced with native plants, which support and sustain new wildlife communities. This gave park ecologists the opportunity to further restore dune landscapes in the area.

Clock Tower Beach

Location: Montreal, Quebec, Canada
Area: 13,000m²
Completion Date: 2012
Landscape Design: CLAUDE CORMIER + ASSOCIÉS INC.
Photography: Claude Cormier + Associés inc. (CC+A), Guillaume Paradis (CC+A), Marc Cramer
Client: Old Port of Montreal Corporation

The introduction of an urban beach to the Quai de l'Horloge is an ideal addition to the recreational and cultural redevelopment project at Montreal's Old Port. A stroll along the quay opens a stunning panorama to the visitor: the mighty St. Lawrence River, the impressive Jacques Cartier Bridge towering over Île Sainte-Hélène, Calder's iconic sculpture, and picturesque Old Montreal as a backdrop to it all.

The project consists of two closely linked components. The first is the creation of an urban beach at Pointe de l'Horloge, with its elegant clock tower built in 1921, and along the lower quay bordering the marina. A huge stairway-ramp makes this convivial venue accessible to all, offering a new and novel approach to city living. Beach umbrellas and weeping willows, brightly colored chairs and fixtures, showers and mist stations, a boardwalk, silky sand, and a refreshment stand all combine to offer visitors a few moments of sheer idleness in a breathtaking setting.

The second component is the parking area, clearly defined by rows of trees that reproduce the triangular layout of the quay. Fed by surface water run-off, the larches, willows, shrub beds, and perennials add cool green ambiance to the space. At the far west end of the site, shooting up from a mound around which a roundabout loops, hundreds of sticks in three shades of blue generate an intriguing pixilation effect. This "porcupine" installation revives a conceptual element emblematic of the firm. And, as an imaginative visual touch, large white thermoplastic dots align to denote each parking spot.

The project, massive yet delightfully simple, extends and intensifies the idea driving the master plan of the Old Port of Montreal to create a "window on the river" by summoning Montrealers and visitors alike to come and enjoy this exceptional site and its atmosphere of leisure and liveliness, recreation and relaxation.

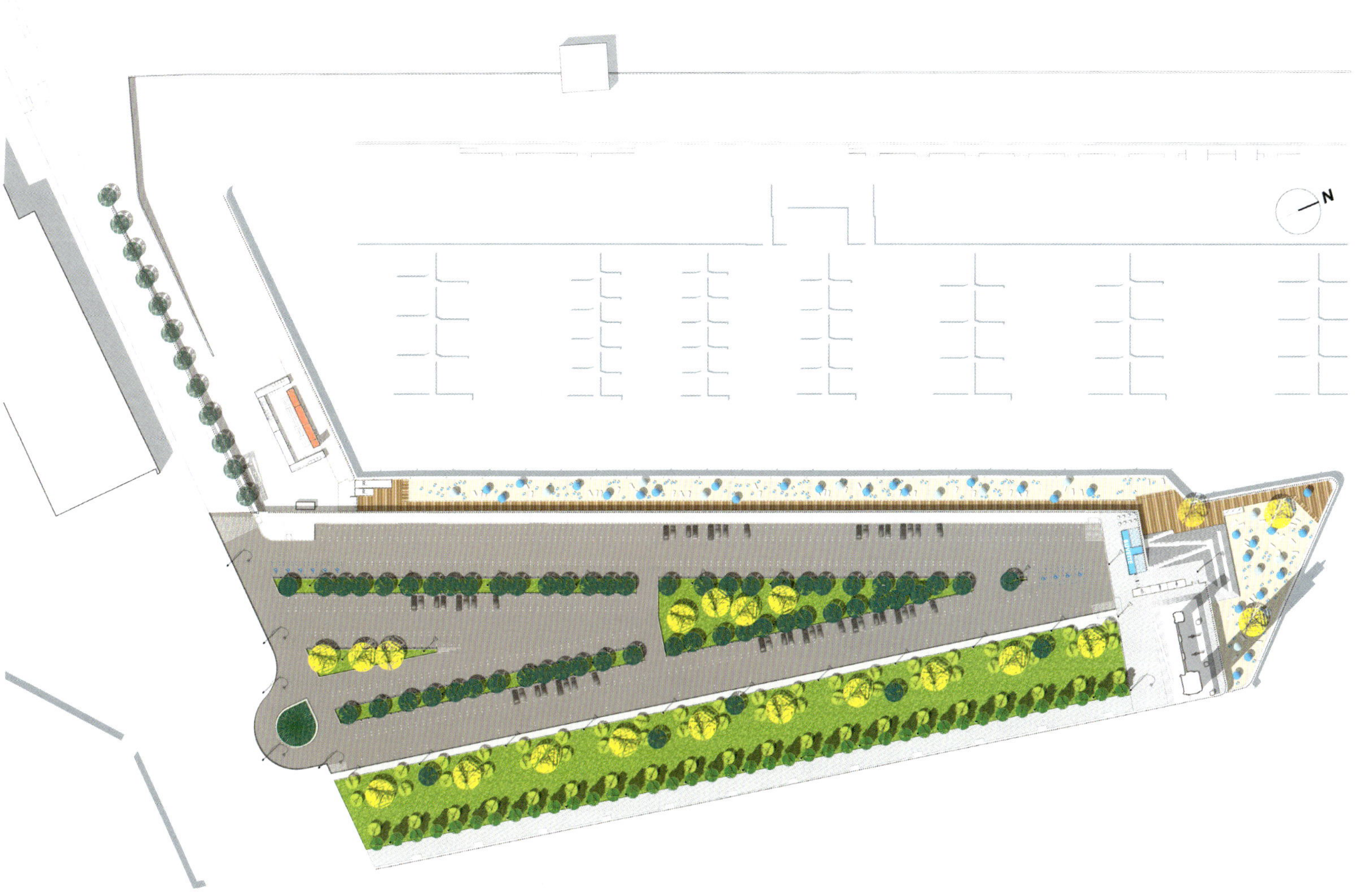

Site Plan

The triangle area for plants surrounded by the paths.

Flowers Distribution Plan

Perennials

Shrubs

Trees

17 Weeping Willows (Salix alba "tristis")
55 Larch (larix decidua)
6 Crab Apples (Malux makamik)

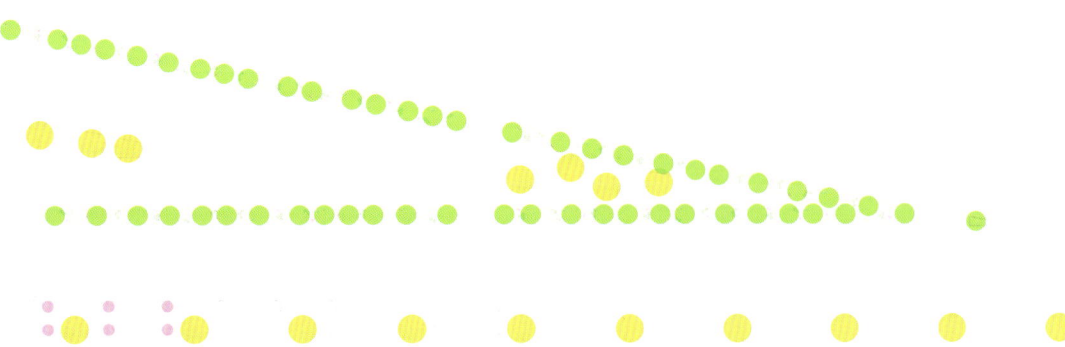

Blue chairs and umbrellas on the beach for rest.

Blue umbrellas in sunshine.

Top: Aerial view image of the triangle beach.

Bottom: The triangle beach with blue umbrellas.

Opposite: The stairs and the beach for rest along the sea.

Chapter 4 Urban Street Design

Streets are the lifeblood of our communities and the foundation of our urban economies. They make up more than 80 percent of all public space in cities and have the potential to foster business activity, serve as a front yard for residents, and provide a safe place for people to get around, whether on foot, bicycle, car, or transit. The vitality of urban life demands a design approach sensitive to the multi-faceted role streets play in our cities.

The purpose of this guide is to standardize street design elements where necessary for consistency and to ensure, as far as it is practical, that minimum requirements are met for efficiency, safety, welfare, convenience, pleasant appearance, environmental sensitivity and economical maintenance.

1. Basic Principles of Urban Street Design

Designing world-class streets begins with a restatement of the problem and the means by which to understand that problem. These four principles establish a clear understanding of the primary goals, ideals and tenets of world-class street design.

1.1 Design Streets for Multiple People

Streets are often the most important, yet underutilized public spaces in cities. The process for planning and designing streets must also be sensitive to both the land use context and to the needs of the various users of a street. Conventional highway design standards tend to focus on streets as thoroughfares for traffic and measure their performance in terms of speed, delay, throughput and congestion. In reality, streets play a much larger role in the public life of cities and communities and should be designed to include public spaces as well as channels for movement. To assure that bicycle, pedestrian and vehicular uses of rights-of-way are the primary uses thereof and that the rights-of-way are properly maintained during construction and repair work in these areas.

1.2 Great Streets are Great for Business

Cities have realized that streets are an economic asset as much as a functional element. Well-designed streets generate higher revenues for businesses and higher values for homeowners.

1.3 Design for Efficiency, Safety, and Convenience

This guide intends to protect the public health, safety, and welfare to the greatest extent possible and minimize inconvenience resulting from construction and maintenance activities within the public right-of-way.

1.4 Streets Can be Changed

Transportation engineers can work flexibly within the building envelope of a street. They can move curbs, change alignments, daylight corners and redirect traffic where necessary. Different types of the streets in the city were created in a different era and need to be reconfigured to meet new needs. Street space can also be reused for different purposes, such as parklets, bicycle parking and pop-up cafés.

2. Basic Elements of Urban Street Design

The elements that make up city streets, from sidewalks to travel lanes to transit stops, all vie for space within a limited right-of-way. Transportation planners and engineers can use this toolbox to optimize the benefits the community receives from its streets.

2.1 Lanes

(1) Parking Lanes

On local streets, any parking lanes provided must be a minimum of seven feet wide, measured from the face of curb. (The parking lane width includes the gutter flag.) Traffic on local streets is relatively low volume and low speed, and most vehicles parked on local streets are passenger autos rather than trucks, so parking lanes are assumed to be narrower than on arterial streets, where parking lanes typically range from eight to ten feet in width, or seven feet if adjacent to a bike lane. In general, width for parking and loading should be provided where there is developed residential frontage on that side of the street, even when required minimum off-street parking is provided, since the on-street parking allows for visitor parking, deliveries, and pick-ups and drop-offs, as well as convenient parking use by residents themselves.

(2) Traffic Lanes

On two-way local streets, traffic lanes should be 10 feet wide, exclusive of parking lane or gutter flag width. Where no parking exists on a particular side of the street, the one-foot gutter flag width is added to the base 10-foot traffic lane width.

On one-way local streets, the single traffic lane is assumed to be 14 feet wide, exclusive of parking lane or gutter flag. Where no parking exists on a particular side of the street, the one-foot gutter flag width is added to the base 14-foot traffic lane width.

The combination of these widths results in a standard roadway width of 34 feet for a two-way street with parking on both sides. Narrower widths require the elimination of parking, or a one-way traffic operation. The minimum nominal one-way street width would be a 16-foot street, with no parking allowed. However, while this width would allow bypass of a stopped vehicle (e.g., loading passengers), it is not recommended for extended distances, since this width might encourage more extensive illegal parking, resulting in difficult movement of traffic during snow conditions or during loading activities. In addition, the Fire Department requires that at least one roadway bordering a residential building be wide enough so that a 10-foot wide fire truck can set jacks down for its aerial ladder. Thus, the minimum width of a local street shall be 22 feet from face-of-curb to face-of-curb for either a two-way street with no parking, or a one-way street with parking on one side. The width of either a two-way street with parking on one side or a one-way street with parking on both sides shall be 28 feet.

On arterial and collector streets, the width of the street pavement is a function of the volume expected to use the roadway and the capacity needed to reasonably accommodate that volume. This determination is made by the Department of Transportation on the basis of traffic studies and volume projections for the preferential street in question.

(3) Bike Lanes

On arterial streets, bike lanes may be striped where the City has determined that a bike lane would be in accordance with the City's Master Plan for Bicycle Routes and where the overall street width and street capacity is adequate to accommodate a bike lane. Generally, a bike lane is a minimum of 5 feet in width. Adjacent parking lanes may be 7 feet in width, and any adjacent vehicular traffic lanes must be a minimum of 10 feet in width.

2.2 Sidewalks

Sidewalks play a vital role in city life. As conduits for pedestrian movement and access, they enhance connectivity and promote walking. As public spaces, sidewalks serve as the front steps to the city, activating streets socially and economically. Safe, accessible, and well-maintained sidewalks are a fundamental and necessary investment for cities, and have been found to enhance general public health and maximize social capital.

Sidewalks shall be provided along all major arterial, arterial and collector streets. Sidewalks shall be a minimum of 4 feet in width on local streets and 5 feet on arterials, collector streets and on local streets with setback sidewalks. In areas with high pedestrian volumes, wider sidewalks may be required. All sidewalks shall be constructed with a maximum cross-slope of 1:50.

As per the related country's Disabilities Act (ADA), a 5-foot by 5-foot passing area must be provided every 200 feet to allow wheelchairs to pass on all sidewalks less than 5 feet wide. Driveways and other connecting sidewalks may be used to provide the passing area, as long as the cross-slope meets ADA standards.

2.3 Transit Streets

Building streets to support transit entails considering every passenger's trip from start to finish. People walking to the transit stop should find their path safe and inviting. Dedicated transit lanes, appropriate base signal timings, and operational traffic improvements ensure that the transit vehicle experiences minimal wait time at intersections and can move freely regardless of traffic congestion, providing a passenger experience competitive with driving. Transit stops also play an important role as part of the streetscape. They have the potential to enhance the quality of the public realm when integrated with certain key features such as quality bus shelters, wayfinding maps, and real-time information systems. Dedicated transit lanes, appropriate base signal timings, and operational traffic improvements ensure that the transit vehicle experiences minimal wait time at intersections and can move freely regardless of traffic congestion, providing a passenger experience competitive with driving.

(1) Dedicated Curbside/Offset Bus Lanes

Dedicated bus lanes are typically applied on major routes with frequent headways (10 minutes at peak) or where traffic congestion may significantly affect reliability. As on-time performance degrades, consider more aggressive treatments to speed transit service. Agencies may set ridership or service standard benchmarks for transitioning bus service to a transit-only facility.

Lanes may be located immediately at the curb or in an offset configuration, replacing the rightmost travel lane on a street where parking is permitted.

(2) Dedicated Median Bus Lanes

Dedicated median bus lanes are typically applied on major routes with frequent headways or where traffic congestion may significantly affect reliability.

Median bus lanes are applied along the centerline of a multi-lane roadway and should be paired with accessible transit stops in the roadway median where needed.

(3) Contra-Flow Bus Lanes

Contra-flow bus lanes are typically applied to bus routes to create strategic, efficient connections rather than as a continuous application along a corridor.

The ideal contra-flow bus lane is designed similar to a regular 2-way street, with non-transit vehicles barred from using the lane or lanes in one direction.

(4) Bus Stops

Bus stop sites shall be chosen such that the areas where lifts or ramps are to be deployed comply with the below requirements. Where provided, bus stop pads shall have a firm, stable and slip resistant surface with a minimum clear length of 96 inches (measured from the face of curb or vehicle roadway edge) and a minimum clear width of 60 inches (measured parallel to the vehicle roadway) to the maximum extent allowed by legal or site constraints.

Newly constructed bus stop pads must provide a square curb surface between the pad and road or other detectable warnings. Bus stop pads shall be at same slope as roadway in the direction parallel to roadway, and maximum 2% slope perpendicular to roadway. Where provided, bus stop shelters shall be installed so as to permit a wheelchair user to enter the shelter from the public way and access a clear floor area of 30 by 48 inches completely within the shelter. Such shelters shall be connected by an accessible route to the boarding area (area where lifts or ramps are to be deployed).

2.4 Stormwater Management

Sustainable stormwater management treats and slows runoff from impervious roadways, sidewalks, and building surfaces. In urban areas, natural drainage patterns have changed over time due to the incremental increase of impervious surface areas. Hardscapes, such as concrete and asphalt, prevent rainfall from being absorbed at the source.

Increased stormwater flows and pollutants enter the subgrade pipe network as a result, burdening the municipal wastewater system (in the case of a Combined Sewer System) or discharging into surface water bodies. High-velocity discharge risks the erosion or flooding of local streams and creeks, destroying natural habitats.

(1) Bioretention

Bioretention consists of an excavated area back-filled with an optional high void ratio crushed stone bottom layer and engineered soil, providing good growing characteristics and high infiltration rates, and planted with woody and/or herbaceous vegetation. In some cases, it can include trees.

Stormwater runoff directed to bioretention will percolate through the engineered soil and stone medium, which provides filtering before infiltration to native soil, or returning through an underdrain to the drainage system. An underdrain is typically placed above the bottom of the crushed stone layer to provide positive drainage once the stone void storage is filled. An overflow mechanism is sometimes included when surface storage is exceeded and overflow to the adjacent roadway or property is not desired.

(2) Porous Pavement

Concrete, asphalt, or paver block surface is constructed so water can flow through the surface and into a storage or infiltration area underneath.

Typical maintenance requirements: vacuuming one to four times a year; performance inspections during rainfall to observe infiltration and general observations (spalling, cracking, missing paver blocks, etc.); inspection of general cleanliness of pavement and surrounding/adjacent landscape every two months during the first year and reduce if performance is meeting expectations; infiltration verification.

Placement of porous pavement can potentially be over the entire areas noted below, or they can be used in partial areas based on traffic patterns, site grading, and tributary area. The areas of placement include local streets, parking lanes (without bus traffic), service drives, alleys, parking lots and sidewalks.

The placement considerations include the following aspects: typically avoid high traffic areas; cautiously select areas with high frequency of starting and stopping, and wheel turning in stationary or slow-moving speeds for porous concrete and porous asphalt applications; adjust snow plowing technique; typically avoid areas with contaminated soils; typically avoid heavy equipment or vehicle traffic (e.g. bus stop); underdrains may be needed; Carefully specify installation requirements, including appropriate weather limitations for porous asphalt and concrete.

(3) Tree Trench

A tree trench consists of an excavated trench back-filled with high void ratio crushed stone, soil, and trees. Water is fed to the tree trenches through infiltration, porous pavement, curb cuts and inlets, or subsurface drainage media. Pretreatment of stormwater through inlets with sumps and filter inserts are good practices to prevent clogging the tree trench media with garbage, debris or excessive sediment in the runoff. Water evaporates, infiltrates, and is filtered of pollutants within the tree trench section. Tree trenches can include underdrains that discharge stormwater to the sewer system if the volume of water delivered to the trench is in excess of its storage and infiltration capacity.

Tree trenches are applicable as stand-alone green street strategies or implemented in combination with porous pavement. Tree trenches could also be installed as an alternative to bioretention. Tree trench installation decisions will need to be made apart from the ODB process through site specific consideration.

3. Urban Street Design Guide

3.1 Intersections

Although all intersections share certain common elements, they are not subject to generalized treatment. To minimize conflicts and provide for anticipated traffic characteristics and designed based on the following factors: traffic factors such as capacities, turning movements, vehicle size and operating characteristics, vehicle speed, pedestrian and bicycle movements, transit operations, and accident history; physical factors such as topography, existing conditions, channelization requirements; and available sight distance; human factors such as driving habits, reaction to surprises, decision and reaction time, and natural paths of movement.

(1) Intersection Design Principles

Whether driving, shopping, walking or lingering, intersections are a focal point of activity and decision, and thus are critical parts of the city streetscape and transportation network. Intersections account for the most serious conflicts between pedestrians, bicyclists, and drivers, but also present opportunities to reduce crashes when designed carefully. Good intersection design can tap civic and economic potential, infusing overbuilt or underutilized spaces with street life. Intersection design should facilitate visibility and predictability for all users, creating an environment in which complex movements feel safe, easy, and intuitive.

Their design should promote eye contact between all street users, engendering a streetscape in which pedestrians, drivers, and bicyclists are aware of one another and can effectively share space. Intersections are the most challenging aspect of street design in an urban environment. Capacity constraints at these pinch points in the roadway network govern the width of roadways as they pass through them. People on foot may avoid difficult crossings or subject themselves or their children to considerable risks while crossing a street at a poorly designed intersection. The principles outlined here enable practitioners to build intersections as meeting points that function well for everyone using them.

(2) Major Intersections

The intersection of two major streets can act as both a barrier and a node. Redesigning major intersections requires designers to critically evaluate the tools and trade-offs available to make an intersection work better for everyone.

While shorter cycle lengths, compact design, and pedestrian safety islands are all desirable components of a multi-modal intersection, the tradeoffs inherent in each make these difficult to achieve simultaneously. Weigh intersection geometry, signal timing, and traffic volumes to formulate a design that clarifies the hierarchy of street users, while enhancing the safety and legibility of the intersection.

(3) Intersections of Major and Minor Streets

Intersections of major and minor streets often lack the same level of definition, safety, and clarity as major intersections. Bicyclists and pedestrians, though legally permitted to cross at these locations, are implicitly discouraged from doing so through design. Vehicles often fail to yield at these locations and have few design cues to suggest they should.

Where major streets meet minor streets, define the transition in street type and context using "gateway" treatments such as curb extensions, raised crossings, and tight curb radii. Use design elements so that people turning from the major to the minor street become aware they are entering a slow speed environment.

(4) Minor Intersections

Raised intersections create a safe, slow-speed crossing and public space at minor intersections. Similar to speed humps and other vertical speed control elements, they reinforce slow speeds and encourage motorists to yield to pedestrians at the crosswalk.

A Roundabout Design Concept Report is to be submitted prior to the approval of any subdivision map or improvement plan that involves the installation of a roundabout. In general, a typical single lane roundabout inscribed diameter of 120 feet is preferred. Detached sidewalks are required. Ideally, a 5-foot landscaped separation and a 10-foot multi-use path is incorporated into the design. Single-lane roundabout speeds, unless located on high-speed corridors or other unusual circumstances, should have entry speeds between 18 to 24 mph.

(5) Complex Intersections

Complex intersections, especially those situated at neighborhood centers or at the junction of several major streets, have tremendous potential to fulfill latent demand for public space. Irregular intersections, which result from successive urban developments and alterations, often occur at the threshold between adjacent grids or where new or preexisting roads cut through the conventional neighbourhood layout. Often overbuilt and confusing, these intersections present safety hazards to all users.

Traffic flow and multi-phase signals result in long delays for pedestrians and cyclists, while at the same time causing confusion among drivers. Acute angled intersections reduce visibility for motorists, while obtuse intersections allow for high-speed turns. Both acute- and obtuse-angled intersections create unnecessarily long pedestrian crossings. Redesign intersections as close to 90 degrees as possible, implementing turn restrictions and street reversals where applicable.

3.2 Intersection Design Elements

Intersections are a critical aspect of street design as the point where motorist, bicycle, and pedestrian movements converge. Successful intersection design addresses all mobility and safety goals as well as opportunities to enhance the public realm. This section explores intersection design and operation, from signal timing to crosswalks, and investigates each concept as it relates to citywide goals for safety, mobility, and more vibrant, accessible public spaces.

(1) Crosswalks and Crossings

Crosswalks are where pedestrians are legally allowed to cross city streets. Marked crosswalks generally consist of two parallel lines perpendicular to the direction of traffic, should align with the edge of right-of-way, and be set back 2 feet from the curb line. Crosswalks must be a minimum of 6 feet in width. Typically, the crosswalk lines are 6 inches in width. In some special applications, such as unsignalized mid-block crossings, a series of 12-inch wide lines parallel to the direction of traffic may be used to delineate the crosswalk, in a so-called International crosswalk pattern.

Crosswalks should be designed to offer as much comfort and protection to pedestrians as possible. Historically, many crosswalks were designed using inadequate, narrow striping, setbacks, deviations from the pedestrian walkway, and considerable crossing distances. Intersection crossings should be kept as compact as possible, facilitating eye contact by moving pedestrians directly into the driver's field of vision.

Midblock crosswalks facilitate crossings to places that people want to go but that are not well served by the existing traffic network. These pedestrian crossings, which commonly occur at schools, parks, museums, waterfronts, and other destinations, have historically been overlooked or difficult to access, creating unsafe or unpredictable situations for both pedestrians and vehicles. Designers should study both existing and projected pedestrian volumes in assessing warrants for midblock crossings to account for latent demand.

A pedestrian crosswalk is a place designated for pedestrians to cross a road. Crosswalks are designed to keep pedestrians together where they can be seen by motorists, and where they can cross most safely across the flow of vehicular traffic.

Marked pedestrian crosswalks are often found at intersections, but may also be at other points on busy roads that would otherwise be too unsafe to cross without assistance due to vehicle numbers, speed or road widths. They are also commonly installed where large numbers of pedestrians are attempting to cross (such as in shopping areas) or where vulnerable road users (such as school children) regularly cross. Rules govern usage of the pedestrian crossings to ensure safety; for example, in some areas, the pedestrian must be more than halfway across the crosswalk before the driver proceeds.

Signalised pedestrian crosswalks clearly separate when each type of traffic (pedestrians or road vehicles) can use the crossing. Unsignalised crosswalks generally assist pedestrians, and usually prioritise pedestrians, depending on the locality. What appear to be just pedestrian crosswalks can also be created largely as a traffic calming technique, especially when combined with other features like pedestrian priority, refuge islands, or raised surfaces.

(2) Traffic Signals

Equally important to the allocation of space, in the form of street cross-sections and geometry, is the allocation of time, performed by traffic signals. Space and time in combination govern how streets operate and how well they provide mobility, safety, and public space. Signal timing is an essential tool, not just for the movement of traffic, but also for a safer environment that supports walking, bicycling, public transportation, and economic vitality.

The operation of a traffic control system should closely mirror a city's policy goals and objectives. Managing traffic signals is important because signals directly impact the quality of the transportation system. While geometric enhancements to a corridor may demarcate space for bikes and buses and create a more multi-modal cross-section, signal timing influences delay, compliance, safety, and mode choice. Traffic signal timing that provides insufficient time for someone to cross the street, for instance, is likely to create an unpleasant experience and may discourage walking entirely. Likewise, significant delays may cause street users to violate the traffic signal or take unsafe risks entering intersections.

Leading Pedestrian Intervals (or LPIs) are a traffic signalization strategy that assigns pedestrians an exclusive 3 to 7 second signal (in some cases much longer) to begin crossing the street before cars get a green light. Consequently, they are also known by their sassier nickname, Pedestrian Head Start.

Signal cycle length is composed of the total signal time to serve all of the signal phases including the green time plus any change interval. Longer cycles will accommodate more vehicles per hour but that will also produce higher average delays. Though often invisible to the public, traffic signal cycle lengths have a significant impact on the quality of the urban realm and consequently, the opportunities for bicyclists, pedestrians, and transit vehicles to operate safely along a corridor. Long signal cycles, compounded over multiple intersections, can make crossing a street or walking even a short distance prohibitive and frustrating. This discourages walking altogether, and makes streets into barriers that separate destinations, rather than arteries that stitch them together.

In general, fixed-time signals are the rule in urban areas for reasons of regularity, network organization, predictability, and reducing unnecessary delay. In certain, less-trafficked areas, actuated signals (push buttons, loop detectors) may be appropriate; however, these must be programmed to minimize delay, which will increase compliance. Actuated signals in general are not preferable because of the maintenance requirements and upkeep of the detection on the street.

Coordinating signals is a method of signal timing that causes systems of signals to work together so that groups of vehicles will be able to move through the signals without stopping. While traditionally applied to increase vehicular traffic flow and reduce peak-hour delay, coordinated signal timing can also be optimized for slower speeds, creating an uninterrupted flow for bicyclists or low vehicle progression speeds for a pedestrian-friendly downtown. Signals may also be timed to coordinate transit headways along routes where regular transit service is consistent and has low variability.

Reference

National Association of City Transportation Officials, NACTO Urban Street Design Guide

City of Chicago, Street and Site Plan Design Standards

City of Milwaukee, Green Streets Stormwater Management Plan

IBK

Location: Innsbruck, Austria
Area: 7500m²
Completion Date: 2011
Landscape Design: AllesWird Gut
Photography: Hertha Hurnaus, Saringer Patrick
Client: Stadt Innsbruck / City of Innsbruck

Maria-Theresien-Straße has always been an important shopping street in direct vicinity to Innsbruck's old town. Although the street is much wider than usual (30m) and therefore has the spatial potential to be an additional square in the city, it has been used in earlier years like an ordinary street with tramway and car traffic in its center.

The main architectural focus of the street and one of the main sights of Innsbruck is Maria-Theresia's column in the center of the space, formerly situated on a traffic island surrounded by cars. The whole space was dominated by its patched up asphalt surface. The space was equipped with a few temporary public seating elements which proved to be very well received by the public. Illumination was suspended from cables crossing the street and thereby obstructing the beautiful and for Innsbruck characteristical view of the mountains.

In 2006 the city of Innsbruck announced a competition for the redesign of Maria-Theresien-Straße. The design and building process was steered by a multiparty committee which consisted of all the necessary authorities of Innsbruck's city council.

The aim of our project was to do justice to the significance that the street has in the townscape of Innsbruck: its goal was to create an urban site with a rich atmosphere that invites strolling, hanging out, and meeting people.

The identity of the site derives from the tension between urbanity and a panoramic view into nature, between past and future, between a specific character and a connective function in the urban structure of Innsbruck.

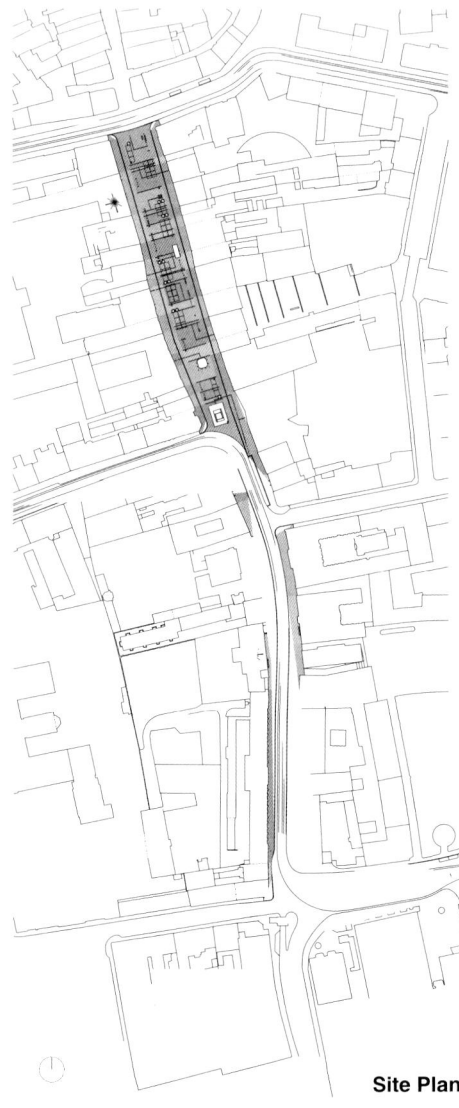

Site Plan

Two defining materials, granite and brass, balance these dualities in the redesigning: a slab carpet of four different types of granite creates a coherent square surface, and a network of brass-colored ground plates with street furniture growing up from it defines the square area proper in the middle of the street.

At night, the walking zones alongside the house façadess are brightly lit, while low-set lighting in the middle of the square enables a view of the mountain silhouette and the stars above.

Today the street has the form of a boulevard: A large public space in the street´s centre contains all the necessary furniture as well as all of the commercially used outdoor seating belonging to the street´s numerous cafés and restaurants. The main historical element of the street, aforementioned Maria-Theresia column, forms the centre of this public space. Two rows of lamp posts mark the border of this space and leave open the view towards the surrounding mountains.

Top: Minimalist-designed bench, garbage bins and docking stations for bikes
Bottom: Minimalist bench
Opposite: The baroque Annasäule

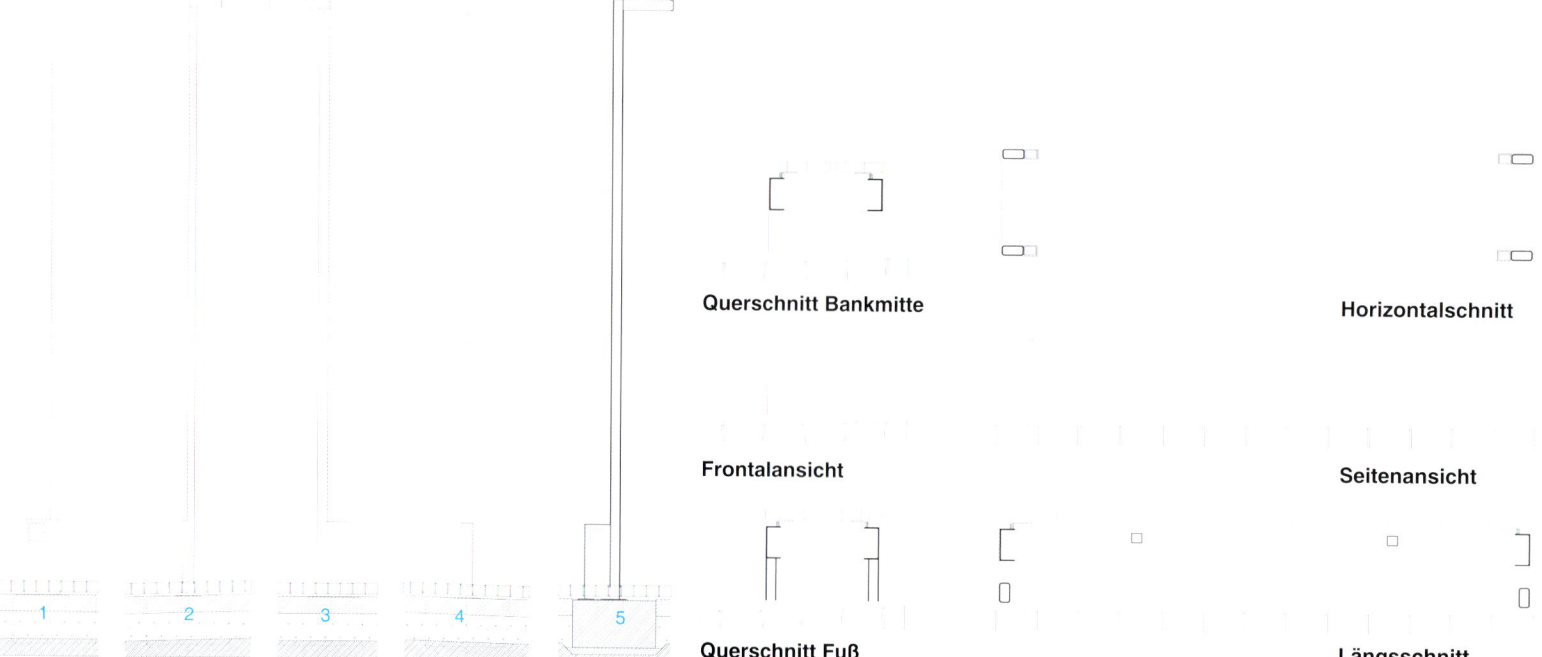

Tall street lamps and floodlights at ground level

1. Seitenansicht 1
2. Frontalansicht Seitenansicht 1
3. Seitenansicht 2
4. Frontalansicht 2
5. Längsschnitt

Querschnitt Bankmitte

Horizontalschnitt

Frontalansicht

Seitenansicht

Querschnitt Fuß

Längsschnitt

Top left: The baroque Annasäule and a street lamp
Top right: St. Jacobs Church and a street lamp
Bottom left: Brass and granite
Bottom right: Golden inlays

Pasing Centre

Location: Munich, Germany
Area: 41300m²
Completion Date: 2014
Landscape Design: TOPOTEK 1
Photography: Hanns Joosten
Client: City of Munich / SWM public services of Munich, MFI Management for real estate Inc

At the western edge of Munich, in a district known as Pasing, a new center is underway. The Pasing train station is one of the most important railway stations in southeastern Germany. The introduction of a new tram line from the centre of Munich and the Pasing Arcaden shopping center facilitated the creation of a new public space; an open square adjoining the train station and a paseo promenade extending east towards the new shopping centre.

The minimal design of the square gives way to a more intimate design strategy for the paseo. In contrast to the square's wide unadorned benches and simplistic gray stone paving, the ground treatment in the paseo is a color-coated asphalt with a floral pattern. An array of platanus trees are planted in the paseo, providing a charming urban space for outdoor strolls. Combined with the high-quality street furnishings, and a play fountain for children, the paseo gives the Pasing district a functional and distinctive public space.

A housing development sits on top of the shopping center, containing several rooftop courtyards. The terraces are open on the south sides, allowing for unimpeded views towards the Alps. They are all designed to create a space that is private and leisurely; wooden decking adjoins the residential units, and communal gathering spaces with children's play areas are situated away from the building.

Paseo with floral pattern

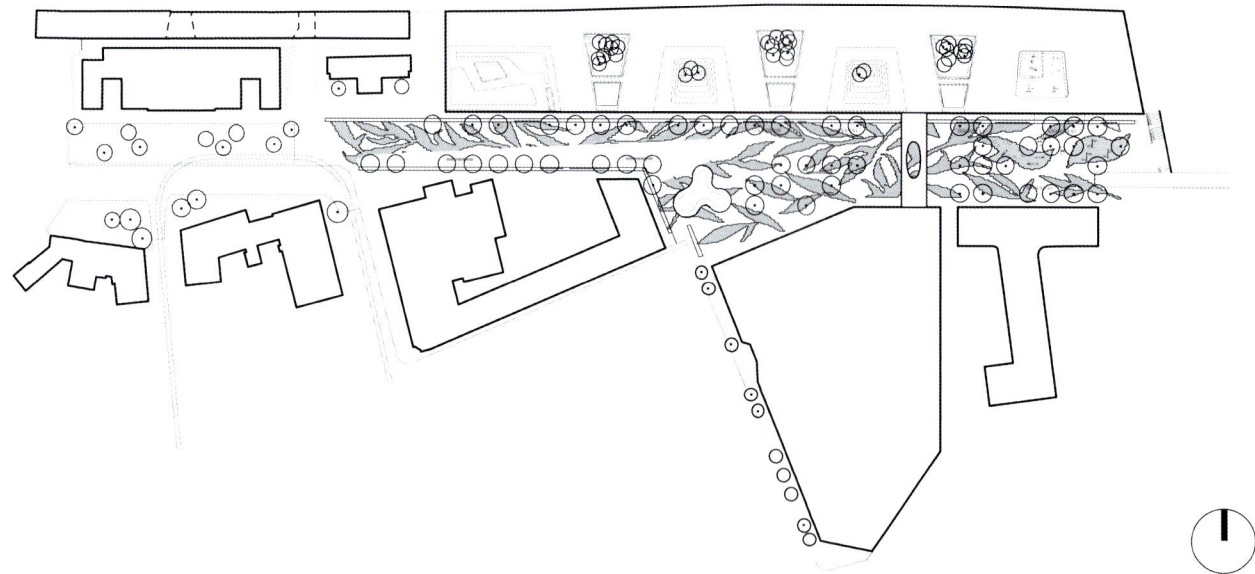

Section of Tree Anchoring

The Paseo - a charming urban space for outdoor strolls

Schematic Plan of Pasing Centre

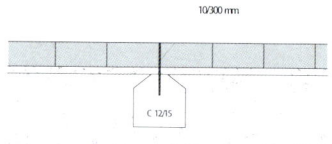

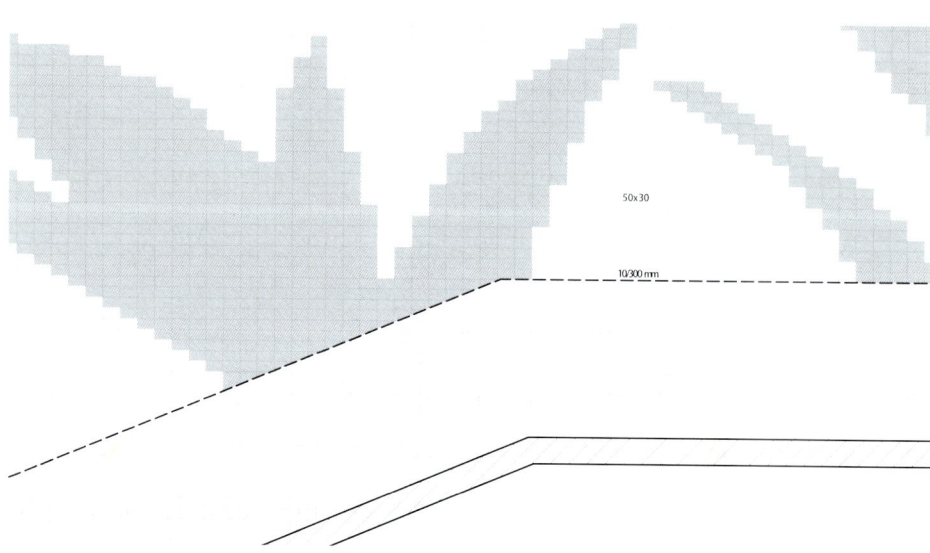

Detail Drawings of Pavement

Opposite: Swings and seesaws on fall protection in contrasting color

237

Parc Hydro-Québec

Location: Montréal, Québec, Canada
Area: 3,260 m²
Completion Date: 2012
Landscape Design: CLAUDE CORMIER + ASSOCIÉS INC.
Photography: Guillaume Paradis Claude Cormier + Associés inc. (CC+A)
Client: Hydro-Québec

Located in the heart of the vibrant Quartier des Spectacles in downtown Montréal, adjacent to the Centre for Sustainable Development, Parc Hydro-Québec unfolds like a pristine forest floor, transplanted into the city and carefully separated from urban pedestrian pressures by a suspended steel grate plaza.

Environmental Sustainability & Adaptive Reuse

Parc Hydro-Québec is a rare example where the entire extent of an urban park is engaged to maximize ecological function.

A rich palette of native understory plants, together with an unevenly distributed grid of 30 canopy trees, covers the 1300-square-meter site. This is a stark transformation, from the site's previous condition as an asphalt parking lot, to a vault of freshness that defines the experience of the park today. In effect, this adaptive re-use decreases storm water runoff from the site by 100% to offset increasing strains on the municipal stormwater system. Heat island effect is diminished by replacing dark, heat absorbing pavement with a nearly contiguous tree canopy cover. It also introduces habitat for birds and insects, through the planting of diverse and native plant species.

The surrounding neighborhood suffers the consequences of heat island effect, exacerbated by the dense downtown context with large paved expanses and significant automobile traffic present throughout the daytime and evening hours. Parc Hydro-Québec

Site Plan
Opposite: The road pavement in white

is a publicly accessible urban oasis intended as an outlet for the thousands of people who work in neighboring office towers. The park is designed to accommodate individual users and small events alike.

Nature in the City

The use of the pervasive suspended steel grate in the design of Parc Hydro-Québec is a tongue-in-cheek play on the ubiquitous tree grates seen throughout downtown Montreal. Completely permeable, this device enables growing conditions comparable to that of a forest, allowing rainwater to flow naturally into the soil while protecting the ground from compaction. It brings the highest level of ecological function into the urban realm in a manner that is contextual, functional and contemporary.

Top & opposite: The white seats in the shape of pentagram on the road

Section Plan

Noosa Junction Station

Location: Noosa Heads, Queensland, Australia
Completion Date: 2011
Architect Design: Bark Design Architects
Photography: Christopher Frederick Jones
Client: Noosa Council

Noosa Junction Station is nestled within rich endemic landscape, Noosa's sense of place is celebrated as an urban design anchor for a developing regional urban precinct; the project is a catalyst for the reinvigoration of the Noosa Junction as a verdant and vibrant public realm. "Place of shade" is the indigenous meaning of Noosa and provides design cues for filtering light and shade with structure and pattern creating an experience of delight and a memorable connection to the natural environment.

The design principles of frames and filigree provide eventual landscape dominant places with low key, filtered and delicate building elements giving transparency and permeability. The project's public amenity as a place for people creates a destination in its own right; its cultural contribution is its vitality and variety of use, providing flexible outdoor rooms for community benefit, interaction and enabling social events.

Contextually the project provides a gradual transition from the vegetation of Girraween "Wetlands" National Park to the two-story forms of the Junction's business center.

Respecting existing pedestrian and cycling paths through the site, the project is considered as a journey through landscape spaces and built form. The recycled timber arbor enhances the long thin site with rhythm and order, with the landscape character changing enroute through the linear sequence of outdoor rooms.

Main Entry

Traditional building technologies kept costs to a minimum and the architectural language of posts, beams, frames, screens, canopies and landscape were economical to define spaces across the site. Concrete, stone, steel, timber and vegetation form the material palette which is robust and durable but warm and natural.

Elements of embedded sustainability are recycled ironbark and tallowwood hardwood from an ex 1930s Mackay wharf, water harvesting for irrigation, endemic drought-tolerant landscape species, locally sourced Queensland spotted gum hardwood, and recyclable steel for durability, low maintenance and future flexibility.

While the design strategies mesh the objectives of both clients, the project delivers a series of subtropical public rooms which give the community a landscape rich "experience" of Noosa's public realm.

Above: Buses take a sweeping arc from the main street and round the key northern point of the building to rest alongside its main pedestrian spine behind and below

Opposite: A wedged roof tilts to the north, pointing to the leisure zones of Noosa Headlands and Beach

Sketch Site Plan

Sketch Perspective

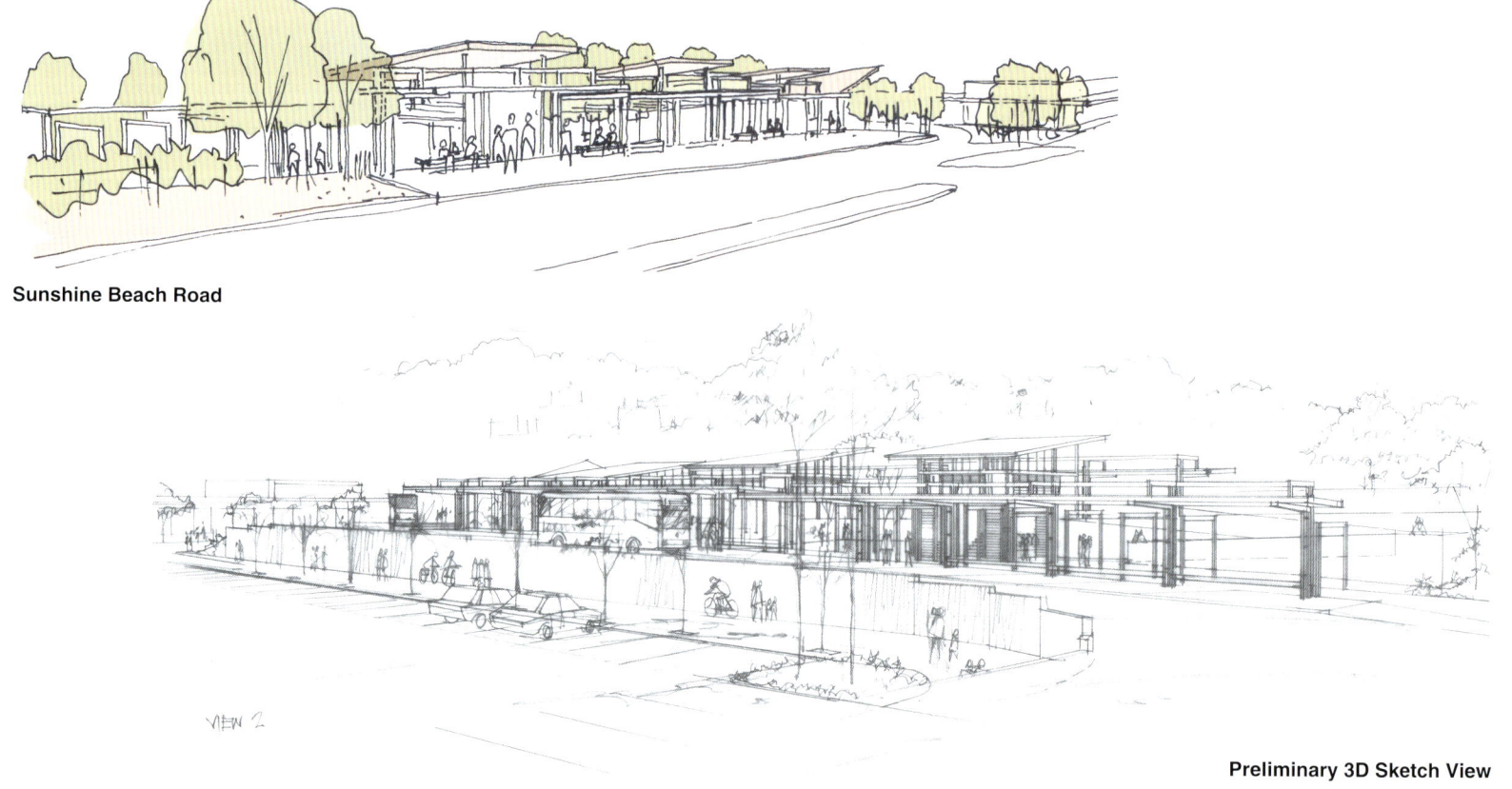

Buses arrive from the road to the east and sweep around the welcome zone to the parking and disembarkation zone on the western side

Sunshine Beach Road

Preliminary 3D Sketch View

Pandanus palm motifs form part of the translucent insert panels in waiting zones

Pandanus Canopy

Gardens are incorporated in the plan, mitigating between eastern and western roads. Circulation spine is made of recycled timber.

Index

Arzu Nuhoglu Landscape Design
Web: www.peyzajtasarim.com
Add: Tarabya Bayırı, Şenevler Girişi No: 52, Tarabya Sarıyer / İstanbul 34457, Turkey
Tel: 90 212 265 37 70-71
Arzu Nuhoglu Landscape Design provides landscape architecture services in a variety of project types in Turkey and the region. The studio led by Arzu Nuhoglu since 1999 amalgamates a broad range of disciplines including landscape architecture, urban design, landscape ecology, engineering and project management. Studio's focus works to establishing the natural and urban values of each project. In their experiences in Turkey and internationally, Landscape Design has played in a variety of roles, ranging from designer to land-use planner to natural conservationists optimizing the scope of each project towards a broad understanding of commercial and public goals. Applying technical and aesthetic skills in urban design, Arzu Nuhoglu's completed projects have been successful in establishing standards for life in Turkey and the region.

Bark Design Architects
Add: Noosa, Queensland, Australia
Tel: 617 5471 0340
Web: www.barkdesign.com.au
Bark is a Sunshine Coast based design practice directed by architects Lindy Atkin and Stephen Guthrie. They have worked together since 1997 after winning a competition to design the Caloundra Regional Art Gallery, which provided the catalyst to establish Bark.
Bark Design Architects are now working through their second decade of design projects in South East Queensland as an energetic and collaborative team of seven people, working from a custom designed Noosa hinterland 'barefoot' studio.
Atkin and Guthrie draw from their international architectural experience, having studied and worked in the USA, Bahamas, London, Melbourne and Sydney. Bark has designed projects in Australia for international clients in Romania, London, Amsterdam, Singapore, Switzerland, Canada and the USA. Projects have been awarded, widely published and exhibited in Australia and internationally.

Bark's design approach carefully considers the landscape, particular microclimates and unlocking the 'spirit' of each site, with projects focused on the broader intention of enhancing people's lives through contemporary design which reveal the essential and nurturing qualities of 'place'.
Like bark, our architecture is an environmental living, growing, and changing skin or structure which offers protection whilst affording our clients a sensitive and inextricable link to the landscape they inhabit.

Claude Cormier + Associes Inc.
Web: www.claudecormier.com
Add: 1223, rue des Carrières, studio A, Montréal (Québec), Canada H2S 2B1
Tel: 514 849 8262
Claude Cormier spent the first twenty years of his life on the family farm in rural Quebec and the past twenty in the city of Montreal. He studied agronomy at Guelph University, Landscape Architecture at the University of Toronto, and History & Theory of Design at Harvard University. In 1995, Cormier founded his Montreal-based landscape design office, which now comprises a team of six diverse landscape architects, all well-travelled individuals. They work on many projects types, from metropolitan planning mandates to temporary installations for garden festivals and everything in between.
Over the past decade, Claude Cormier Architectes Paysagistes has produced an iconic body of work that has been recognized nationally and internationally. Cormier was selected as an Emerging Voice for North America by the Architectural League of New York, and his firm's projects have garnered honours from organizations that include the American Society of Landscape Architects, the Canadian Society of Landscape Architects, the Montreal Institute of Design, Heritage Montreal, and the Quebec Association of Landscape Architects.

C. F. Møller Architects
Web: www.cfmoller.com
Add: C.F. Møller Danmark A/S, Europaplads 2, 11. 8000 Aarhus C, Danmark
Tel: 45 8730 5300
C.F. Møller is one of Scandinavia's oldest and largest architectural practices. Their award-winning work involves a wide range of expertise that covers all architectural services, landscape architecture, product design, healthcare planning and management advice on user consultation, change management, space planning, logistics, client consultancy and organisational development. Simplicity, clarity and unpretentiousness, the ideals that have guided their work since the practice was established in 1924, are continually re-interpreted to suit individual projects, always site-specific and based on international trends and regional characteristics.
C.F. Møller regard environmental concerns, resource-consciousness, healthy project finances, social responsibility and good craftsmanship as essential elements in their work, and this holistic view is fundamental to all their projects, all the way from master plans to the design.
Today C.F. Møller has app. 350 employees. Their head office is in Aarhus, Denmark and we have branches in Copenhagen, Aalborg, Oslo, Stockholm and London.

Debarre Duplantiers Associés
Web : www.debarreduplantiers.com
Add: 13 Boulevard de Rochechouart - 75009 Paris, France
Tel: 33 01 42 81 48 42
Debarre Duplantiers Associés is a multidisciplinary office for metropolitan studies. The firm is comprised of three poles, architecture, urban planning and landscape design, that work much like a pair of 3D glasses : the desired effect is only achieved when both lenses are working in unison.
This consubstantial interaction forms a foundation from which all of the firm's projects are based. The natural and built environments therefore have a more porous border between the two, and the resultant interpretation of works is unique, due to this binary vision.

DIGITALEpaysage
Web: www.digitalepaysage.com
Add: 39 rue de l'école, 67330 Imbsheim France
Tel: 33 (0)3.88.71.37.68
The DIGITALEpaysage studio was established in 2007 by Agnès Daval. The company associates experiences of his leader and those of Bruno

Steiner town planner and graduate in architecture, landscape architect, partner since 2008.
This binomial "landscape" proposes a strong complementarity of skills. The know-how of DIGITALEpaysage, acquired in 15 years of experience, touch all the types of landscape (ruraland urban natural spaces) and all the scales.

DLC Architects
Web: www.dlcarchs.com
Add: Mexico City, Mexico
Tel: 0152 (55) 55624552
DLC was born in 2004, México City by founding partners; Arch. María Domínguez Landa and Arch. Rafael López Corona, with the vision of creating an interdisciplinary studio, committed with aesthetic and environmental principles on every challenge their clients entrust them.
The company is specialized in 3 major areas:
Visualization; For them is not only a word, it represents a whole new way of thinking, either working with real state companies and architecture firms of worldwide recognition to developing images for their "in house" projects. From hospitality to retail, from furniture to urban developments, THEY generate artistic images that always try to expand and accent the assets in every project.
Architecture; Architects, landscapers, designers and urban planners come together to conceptualize, design, construct and supervise every type of project, either residential, corporate, interior, retail or landcape and urban. Their philosophy blurs the edges between design, architecture and landscape in order to integrate them into an excecutive document, with technical, sustainable, construction and branding specifications.
Design; Consists on the creative and techincal process lead to come up with strategies involving graphical, useful and aesthetic expressions in any way, i.e. architecture, graphic and industrial design.

DS Architecture – Landscape
Web: www.dsmimarlik.com
Add: Kuloğlu Mh. Başağa Çeşmesi Sk, No: 13 34433 Beyoğlu / İstanbul TR, Turkey
Tel: 0212 245 57 12
Being a pioneer in its field since 15 years, DS is a design office that has both theoretical and practical products on where architecture and landscape intersect. The main goal of the works is to create sustainable, practicable, well designed places with something to tell.
DS designs have the "setting of a microcosmos" as the main motivation. The design group perceives the complex fabric of today's multilayered, multicultural and interdisciplinary environment as a source and using this source, it sets up meaningful, clear, creative new places with the motto of combining high artistical skills with rational, economic and ethical values; both in national and international projects. Considering nature as another source, the group creates parametrical designs thorough a sentactical perception of nature by filtering it.
DS provides design services ranging in scale from residential and urban projects, cooperating with distinguished architects, planners, engineers and especially ecologists.

Fitzgerald Frisby Landscape Architecture
Web: ffla.com.au
Add: Level 4, 700 Collins Street, Docklands Victoria 3008, Australia
Tel: 613 9670 9900
Fitzgerald Frisby Landscape Architecture provides landscape architectural and urban design consulting services across a diverse range of project type sand scales for both public and private clients.
The following provide general guiding principles regarding the FFLA approach to projects: Community engagement should help to set the agenda for the design process, and provide inspiration to it. Design must strive for deeper outcomes than the visual appeal of patterns, shapes and forms. It should seek to create connections to community and place, working with the stories and people that exist rather than smothering the old with the new. Sustainability needs to go beyond words to provide real and measurable results if it is to meet the challenges faced by contemporary society. Experimenting with new processes and techniques ensures that design remains interesting and informed. Research as a part of the design process in provides an insight to the evolution of place and an appreciation of local stories. Collaborating with the community and other professionals can provide valuable insights to local issues as well as solutions to complex problems. Community collaboration is a valuable means of achieving lasting outcomes. Outcomes of the design process must be practical and robust. They should be good value, valued and valuable.

G & C Arquitectos
Web: www.gc-arquitectos.com
Add: Bizkaia, Spain
Tel: 94 497 13 84
G&C ARQUITECTOS, founded in 1997, is an architectural firm which specializes in architecture, urban planning, and landscaping.
Some of its standout projects include designing and landscaping the Bake Eder parcel, Zelaieta Park, Herriko Square and its surroundings in Amorebieta-Etxano, and Atalaia Park in Armintza, Lemoiz, all of which were the result of public design competitions. They recently won, in conjunction with JDVDP Architects, the Zorrozaurre green areas and outdoor spaces international competition in Bilbao which was based on the Master plan of Zaha Hadid.
Their professional development has been focused on landscaping, urban renewal, and both civic and corporate architecture. The G&C Architects is founded by Marta González Cavia, Martin González Cavia, and Jorge Cabrera Bartolomé.

JDS / JULIEN DE SMEDT ARCHITECTS
Web: jdsa.eu
Add: Kompagnistræde 29, 1208 Copenhagen, Denmark
Tel: 45 3378 1010
JDS / Julien De Smedt Architects is a multidisciplinary office that focuses on architecture and design, from large scale planning to furniture. Rich with multiple expertises, the office is fuelled by talented designers and experienced architects that jointly develop projects from early sketches to on-site supervision. All of which, regardless of scale, outlines an approach that is affirmatively social in its outcome, enthusiastic in its ambition and professional in its process. At the core of our architecture is the ability to take a fresh look at design issues through experienced eyes. Their approach aims at turning intense research and analysis of practical and theoretical matters into the driving forces of design. By continuously developing rigorous methods of analysis and execution, JDS is able to combine innovative thinking and efficient production.

Founded and directed by Julien De Smedt (co-founder of PLOT), JDS currently employs some 30 people with offices in Copenhagen, Brussels and Shanghai. They work with corporate, government and private clients in numerous countries to realize major civic, hotel, residential, office, commercial, health care, educational, and waterfront developments. They carefully limit the commissions they take on to help ensure a high degree of professional attention and overall project quality. JDS envisions itself as a proactive partner for its client, rather than a consultant. The office has a wide portfolio of international work and the attitude of involving external consultants to improve the design intelligence of a given project team. The use of complementing teams ensures that a project will never suffer from being neither too conventional nor too naive.

Karres en Brands landscape architecture + urban planning
Web: karresenbrands.nl
Add: Oude Amersfoortseweg 123 1212 AA Hilversum,The Netherlands
Tel: 31 35 642 29 62
Karres and Brands is an international design office for landscape architecture and urban planning. The office was founded in 1997 by Sylvia Karres and Bart Brands, and works on a very wide range of projects, studies and design competitions in the Netherlands and abroad. Their work encompasses all levels of scale and all aspects of the public domain.

Martha Schwartz Partners
Web: www.marthaschwartz.com
Add: 65-69 East Road, London N1 6AH, United Kingdom
Tel: 44 (0)20 7549 7497
Martha Schwartz Partners (MSP) is a leading international design practice whose work focuses on activating and regenerating urban sites and city centres. Situated at the intersection of landscape, art, and urbanism, Martha Schwartz Partners has over 30 years of experience designing and implementing installations, gardens, civic plazas, parks, institutional landscapes, corporate headquarters, master plans, and urban regeneration projects. MSP works with city leaders, planners and builders at a strategic level so as to advocate for the inclusion of the public landscape as a means to achieve environmental, economic, social and environmental sustainability. MSP's work demonstrates a deep commitment to the urban landscape as it performs as the platform for sustainable cities that are healthy across all aspects, sectors, and domains of urban life.
With offices in the United Kingdom, the United States and China, Martha Schwartz Partners is engaged in projects and consultation around the globe and has to date worked on projects in over 20 countries and four continents.

OKRA
Web: www.okra.nl
Add: OKRA landschapsarchitecten bv Oudegracht 23, 3511 AB Utrecht, The Netherlands
Tel: 31 (0)30 27 34 249
OKRA is an award-winning design office for landscape architecture and urbanism. Over the last twenty years OKRA has focused on the transformation of cities and landscapes for the people who use them. OKRA has extensive experience in defining frameworks for urban development, design public space, master planning and strategies. OKRA is a multi-disciplinary team with more than 20 international professionals working enthusiastically with partners and clients to create a better environment.

Rios Clementi Hale Studios
Web: www.rchstudios.com
Add: 639 N. Larchmont Blvd, Suite 100, Los Angeles, CA 90004, United States
Tel: (323) 785-1800
Rios Clementi Hale Studios was founded in 1985 as a multi-disciplinary design firm. They create singular, integrated and comprehensive solutions for a variety of design challenges. Combined, their talents comprise a wide range of professional skills including architecture, landscape architecture, urban planning and design, interior design, graphics and signage, exhibit and product design. Project types include commercial, residential, civic, educational, institutional, exhibits and product and furniture design.
They are dedicated to applying a strong interdisciplinary collaborative approach to the design process, whether on projects within their office or in consultation with other design firms. A broad mixture of clients and projects has given them solid experience in dealing with various and complex design issues.
They are committed to exploring new design opportunities which are specific to the spirit and mission of each project. This goal is achieved on a variety of scales and through various disciplines to create design solutions that fulfill and even exceed our client's expectations.

Rush\Wright Associates
Web: www.rushwright.com
Add: Level 4, 105 Queen Street, Melbourne 3000, Australia
Tel: 61.3.9600.4255
Rush\Wright Associates is an award winning design practice based in Melbourne, Australia, offering consultancy services in landscape architecture, urban design and constructed ecology. Bringing together the extensive experience and design expertise of its Directors Catherine Rush and Michael Wright, the company has built its reputation on commitment to client service and innovative design outcomes.
They have extensive experience working with private and public sector client authorities, as well as federal, state, and local government bodies in the design evolution and delivery of landscape and urban design projects at the complete range of scales. Their work internationally includes collaborations with offices in the United States, United Kingdom, New Zealand and the United Arab Emirates. In Australia, they are currently working in Victoria, Tasmania, the Australian Capital Territory and in New South Wales. In Asia, they are working in Vietnam, Laos and China.
As a design practice, they offer a unique combination of services, focused on marrying client expectations with the best possible design solution and environmental principles. They have a demonstrated track-record in designing landscapes and urban design proposals that go beyond

superficial formal gestures to embrace sustainability, community values and the new environmental agenda. These are vital issues for their time.

Studio 3LHD
Web: www.3lhd.com
Add: Nikole Božidarevića 13/4, 10000 Zagreb, Croatia
Tel: 385 1 2320200
3LHD is a collaborative architectural studio, particularly interested in the integration of architecture, art and (urban) landscape, an approach which has resulted in a series of projects and realizations in Croatia and abroad. 3LHD has an integrative approach to projects and believes that in addition to functional, architecture must respond to many other issues. Basic principles of the practice are woven into the modernity of the early 21st century.

Their design approach is each time with different realities, and with many different parameters that they give themselves and which are given to them, it is integral, analytical and iterative. It is based on modification of opinions of different people, that they seek to bring into production, these are various specialists, experts in various areas and with them they try to achieve highest quality. This is where their approach is like that of a producer and they often bring themselves in the role of a director or a DJ who performs the best editing. In such a way they investigate the most appropriate concept and try to create new value. They always make a kind of a prototype, which is sometimes, like in automobile industry, a redesign, and sometimes a research undertaking.

Surfacedesign, Inc.
Web: www.sdisf.com
Add: 12 Decatur Street San Francisco, CA 94103, United States
Tel: 415.621.5522
Surfacedesign, Inc. was established in 2001 to provide clients with a broad range of professional design services, including landscape architecture and urban design and master planning. The award-winning practice is engaged in projects of a variety of different scales, both locally and internationally: estate design, park design, hospitality, corporate campuses, municipal streetscapes, and large-scale land use planning and urban design projects. They create projects that have a strong relationship to people and the natural environment, they are passionate about craftsmanship and sustainability.

TOPOTEK 1
Web: topotek1.de
Add: Gesellschaft von Landschaftsarchitekten mbH, Sophienstrasse 18, 10178 Berlin, Germany
Tel: 49-30-2462580
TOPOTEK 1 was founded in Berlin in 1996 by Martin Rein-Cano. It works around the field of landscape architecture and understands itself as a traveler within the fringe areas of typologies and scales, jaunting into architecture, urban design, music and art. The hybridisation of topics and disciplines, the removal, transmission and re-contexualisation of various design features and objects, and the staging and design of scenographic sequences are just some of their key strategies.

The alertness and receptivity to the general contemporary discussion is maintained through this working method. The goal movement of society and culture continually redefines the broad spectrum of possibilities in relation to the constitution of public space.

TOPOTEK 1 develops concepts through a critical understatement of the given realities and a deep historical knowledge. This provides solutions and designs which fulfill the modern requirements of variability, communication and sensuality.

Urbicus
Web: www.urbicus.fr
Add: 3, Rue Edme Fremy, 78000 Versailles, France
Tel: 01 39 53 14 35
Urbicus has carried out all kinds of projects for regional development at various locations and contrasting sites since it was founded by Jean-Marc Gaulier in 1996. The agency of about fifteen associates works to transform landscapes whose public or private organizations entrust the work to them. Urbicus, experimented with the consequences of civility projected in nature and nature projected in towns. In Architectes x paysagisted, the x is the botanical symbol for hybridization. It is theirmethodological signature. It represents the intersection of skills and the cross-cutting approach of the reflection applied to their projects and necessary for a modern-day approach to land development issues. As town planners, architects and landscape architects, they approach the landscape as a relevant way of tackling urban issues.

Vladimir Balda
Add: Chrastava,Czech Republic
E-mail: vladimir@balda.biz
www.balda.biz
Vladimir balda is the architect born in 1972, graduated from the Faculty of Architecture.At the same time,he is a teacher working at the Faculty of Architecture at TU Liberec. He is interested in projects of public spaces and residential buildings. His famous project has ever received Think Arch first prize for architects under forty years of age and the Grand Prix 2013-National Prize of architecture.

Zur Wolf Landscape Architects
Web: www.zur-wolf.com
Add: 103 Medinat Hayehudim St., P.O.B 330, Herzliya, 46103, Israel
Tel: 09-9510020
Zur Wolf Landscape Architects is an award-winning international office for urban design and landscape architecture, founded in 1953, by the landscape Architects Lipa Yahalom & Dan Zur. Over the last 60 years they have established themselves as a leading practice with a team of 16 landscape architects and designers. On 1998 Lipa Yahalom & Dan Zur received the prestigious "Israel Prize" for their contribution on the field of Landscape Architecture. Lior Wolf became partner on 2006 and owns the office since 2011.

With a multi-disciplinary approach to complex design issues, Zur-Wolf has extensive experience in large-scale urban master planning and design, urban parks, national parks, Institutions, campuses, landscape interventions, neighborhoods, streets, squares and gardens. They believe in planning that is driven from the site and reacts to it, with an innovative approach, original and fresh, in high quality and modesty.